MARCH TO
REDEMPTION

Jonathon Gruenke

The Virginian-Pilot | Daily Press

Jonathon Gruenke

No part of this publication may be reproduced, stored in a retrieval system or transmitted in any form by any means, electronic, mechanical, photocopying or otherwise, without prior written permission of the publisher, Triumph Books LLC, 814 North Franklin Street; Chicago, Illinois 60610.

This book is available in quantity at special discounts for your group or organization.
For further information, contact:

Triumph Books LLC
814 North Franklin Street
Chicago, Illinois 60610
Phone: (312) 337-0747
www.triumphbooks.com

Printed in U.S.A.
ISBN: 978-1-62937-660-8

The Virginian-Pilot and Daily Press
Jami Frankenberry, Greg Giesen, Ryan Gilchrest, Jonathon Gruenke, Jonathan Heeter, The' Pham,
Erica Smith, Adrin Snider, David Teel and Norm Wood

Content packaged by Mojo Media, Inc.
Joe Funk: Editor
Jason Hinman: Creative Director

Front and back cover photos by Jonathon Gruenke

Except where otherwise noted, all interior photos by AP Images.

CONTENTS

INTRODUCTION

By David Teel

Virginia was on the brink of college basketball's pinnacle when Ralph Sampson, the man who first carried the program to a Final Four, rose from his courtside seat and urged Cavaliers faithful to be heard. Heard they were. And heard this destined-for-documentary story of redemption will be for generations.

Virginia is your 2019 national champion.

Humbled and ridiculed a year ago by a historic NCAA tournament loss, the Cavaliers defeated Texas Tech 85-77 in an overtime classic at U.S. Bank Stadium.

During the final four minutes of regulation and throughout overtime, every possession, shot and pass, heck every dribble, oozed tension. Neither team would break. Too much talent, too much heart.

Twice Virginia led by 10, and with 5:46 remaining in the second half, its margin was 59-51. But y'all didn't think this would be easy, did you?

Fate was absolutely not going to let the Cavaliers' breathtaking postseason end casually. So, Texas Tech scored eight consecutive points, forging a 59-all tie on Norense Odiase's 3-point play.

With less than a minute remaining in regulation, the Red Raiders took their first second-half lead, 66-65, on Jarrett Culver's layup, and Odiase's two free throws extended the margin to 68-65.

But off an XL assist from Ty Jerome, De'Andre Hunter buried a right-corner 3-pointer to force OT at 68.

The teams then exchanged the lead until another Hunter 3-pointer gave the Cavaliers a lead they would not relinquish.

Hunter scored a career-high 27 points, 22 after a skittish first half. Kyle Guy, the Final Four's Most Outstanding Player, added 24. Meanwhile, Brandone Francis and Matt Mooney kept Texas Tech close with big shot after big shot.

But five Cavaliers — Guy, Hunter, Jerome, Mamadi Diakite and Braxton Key — combined to make 12 of 12 free throws in OT. Overtime perfection in suffocating pressure.

"We've got some dudes who've got some onions," associate head coach Jason Williford said.

It was with 11:24 left in regulation that Sampson, the three-time national Player of the Year and leader of Virginia's 1981 Final Four group, stood and implored more noise. As if that were possible.

After all, noise has followed Virginia since last season's first-round NCAA loss to UMBC, the first by a No. 1 seed to a No. 16.

Coach Tony Bennett leaned on many people and devices to motivate and heal himself and his team in the UMBC aftermath. None resonated more Monday night than a 44-year-old letter Bennett shared with the Cavaliers.

Iconic coach Clair Bee wrote the letter of encouragement to then-Indiana coach Bob Knight after Knight's undefeated Hoosiers lost to Kentucky in the 1975 tournament.

Kyle Guy celebrates after Virginia's historic national championship win over Texas Tech. (Photo by Jonathon Gruenke)

"Take a deep breath, get your bearings, set your sights on even greater heights and start all over again," Bee began. "All a frustrated young man can expect to see as he looks over his shoulder is a desolate cemetery where his broken dreams lie buried in defeat."

One year later, Indiana went 32-0, and those Hoosiers remain the sport's last unblemished national champion.

Bennett's Cavaliers also responded to their crushing disappointment admirably, winning the ACC regular season for the fourth time in six years. But what of the postseason?

The Final Four brought partial closure. But why not more? Why not win two more games and bring the story full circle?

That the Cavaliers did, with a mind-bending comeback against Auburn on Saturday and Monday's conquest.

"I don't know of anything else that would allow these guys to be able to handle this situation, to play through stuff and to have a perspective and a poise and a resiliency unless they went through something that hard," Bennett said of UMBC. "They're … really good players. They don't probably get enough credit — well, I think some of them do for their talent — but they had something different about them collectively."

Bennett will never view it as such, but the championship is complete vindication, for his program, defense-first system and, most important, the young men who returned from last year.

Guy, Jerome and Hunter. Diakite, Jack Salt and Jay Huff.

They were resilient and gracious in defeat. They were strong and humble in victory.

Lack of major-league franchise aside, our state has long been graced with enduring teams and athletes. But this Monday night in Minneapolis, with its burning spotlight and international audience, was different.

The closest comparison is Jan. 4, 2000, in New Orleans, where, the Y2K scare in the rearview mirror, Virginia Tech played Florida State in the Sugar Bowl for college football's national championship. Michael Vick and the Hokies lost that evening but joined with the Seminoles for a riveting show.

Among college basketball's fiercest defenses, Virginia and Texas Tech weren't likely to produce similar pyrotechnics. But they did, and spare us the hand-wringing over the matchup lacking a blueblood program or No. 1 NBA draft pick sure to draw record TV ratings.

Expertly coached and stocked with skilled, team-first players, the Cavaliers and Red Raiders deserved to be here. Indeed, they earned their way with stirring regular seasons and tournament runs.

Texas Tech defeated four top-15 teams in succession — Buffalo, Michigan, Gonzaga and Michigan State — to reach the final. Virginia bested eight ranked opponents during the regular season, five on the road, before dismissing two others — Purdue and Auburn — with indelible tournament finishes.

Sure, Duke-Kentucky or another clash of storied programs, would have had broader appeal. But elite college basketball today extends far beyond traditional borders, and never was it more evident than Monday night when Virginia authored the most stirring moment in the commonwealth's sports annals and a college basketball epic for the ages.

"One of our themes, I told them before the Auburn game: Just bring your two fish and your five loaves — that's a story in the Bible," Bennett said. "I said, 'It will be enough. It will be enough for the masses. When you guys play the right way, the collectiveness of it takes over.' And I've watched it and stepped back and I've seen them mature through everything. For them to do what they did and how they've won, it's a great story. It really is." ∎

Ty Jerome (left) and Kyle Guy played huge roles in capturing the title for U.Va., with Jerome contributing 16 points, six rebounds and eight assists, and Guy scoring 24 points. (Photo by Jonathon Gruenke)

NCAA Tournament National Championship

Virginia 85, Texas Tech 77 (OT)
April 8, 2019 • Minneapolis, Minnesota

HOW SWEET IT IS!

U.Va. wins first NCAA basketball title in instant classic

By Norm Wood

One. More. Time.

Virginia showed resolve to bounce back from a 14-point first-half deficit in the first round against Gardner-Webb, kept Oregon at arm's length in the Sweet 16, withstood Purdue's best in the Elite Eight and survived Auburn's resilience in the national semifinal. Yet, there the Cavaliers were Monday night, facing overtime in the national championship game after a late rally by Texas Tech.

One. More. Time.

Again, U.Va. had what it took down the stretch and wouldn't be denied in its quest to make a 180-degree turn in the NCAA tournament.

An 85-77 overtime win against Texas Tech ensured U.Va.'s ultimate comeback after last season becoming the first No. 1 seed in tournament history to lose to a No. 16 seed, when the Cavaliers fell to UMBC in the first round.

Claiming the first men's basketball national championship in school history was the sweetest redemption of all.

"You guys faced pressure that no team in the history of the game has faced, well, really all year," U.Va. coach Tony Bennett said, addressing guards Kyle Guy, De'Andre Hunter and Ty Jerome on the interview dais after the game. "Being down 14 against Gardner-Webb, and you did not panic in the moment, and you fought

and you found a way out. That, I think, has prepared you for this moment to be able to handle the pressure or the intensity of a national championship game."

Hunter, who scored 22 of his game-high 27 points after halftime and made a crucial 3-pointer in the final minute of regulation to tie the game, knocked down another 3-pointer with 2:09 left in overtime to put the Cavaliers ahead 75-73 — a lead they wouldn't relinquish.

Making all 12 of its free throws in overtime, U.Va. (35-3) made sure Texas Tech wouldn't have a chance to claw its way back into the game, like it had in regulation. Guy, who finished with 24 points, made four free throws in the last 2:45 of overtime.

Hunter missed seven of eight shots from the floor in the first half, but he flipped those results the rest of the game, connecting on seven of his last eight shots.

"I was aggressive in the first half, I believe, but my shots just weren't falling," said Hunter, who also had nine rebounds. "I just tried to do the same thing in the second half, and my shots were falling. Just staying aggressive, that's it."

Jerome scored eight of his 16 points in the second half to accompany his game-high eight assists. Texas Tech had five players score in double figures, led by Brandone Francis' 17 points off the bench.

Trailing 59-51 with under five minutes left in the second half after Hunter followed a Guy miss with a

Kyle Guy put together a masterful shooting performance, hitting 8-of-15 shots from the floor, including 4-of-9 on 3-pointers for 24 points. (Photo by Jonathon Gruenke)

stickback, Texas Tech looked to be on the verge of fading out with a whimper.

Not quite.

Similar to Saturday night's national semifinal when U.Va. led Auburn 57-47 with 5:22 left before the Tigers went on a 14-0 run and U.Va. had to rally for a dramatic 63-62 win, the Cavaliers had trouble holding on to a late cushion against the Red Raiders.

Texas Tech's 8-0 run tied the game 59-59. The teams went back and forth in the closing minutes of regulation, before the Red Raiders took a 68-65 lead with 22 seconds remaining on a pair of free throws by Norense Odiase.

That's when Hunter came up huge, preserving Virginia's season via a 3-pointer off a feed from Jerome with 14 seconds left in front of the Cavaliers' bench to tie the game 68-68 and send it to OT.

It was the eighth championship game to end in overtime, and the culmination of a postseason of pressure

Opposite: The journey from first-round NCAA loss in 2018 to national championship in 2019 was a long one but made the first title in program history that much more meaningful. Above: Tony Bennett celebrates the championship with his team, completing an amazing turnaround of the program in his 10 years as head coach. (Photos by Jonathon Gruenke)

moments successfully navigated by the Cavaliers.

"We came in together and said that we were going to win a national championship," said Guy, referring to himself and Jerome. "To be able to hug each other with confetti going everywhere and say we did it, it's the greatest feeling I've ever felt in basketball."

The closing minutes of regulation and overtime stood in sharp contrast to the game's slow outset — not an entirely unexpected start for programs that entered the night with two of the top three scoring defenses in the nation.

Typically glacial in terms of tempo in the early going, both teams got off to a less-than-scintillating start on the offensive end, but Texas Tech couldn't find any open shots against U.Va.'s pack-line defense.

U.Va. forced Texas Tech (31-7) to work the ball around in the half-court to try to get an open look in the first 10 minutes, as the shot clock routinely dipped under three seconds for the Red Raiders.

Opposite: De'Andre Hunter elevates for the shot while surrounded by Texas Tech defenders. Hunter dominated the game on both sides of the ball and had his best performance of the tournament on the biggest stage with 27 points and nine rebounds. Above: U.Va. fans had plenty to celebrate in Minneapolis, witnessing their team's historic championship win. (Photos by Jonathon Gruenke)

Despite Texas Tech opening the game by missing its first nine shots from the floor, U.Va.'s lead was just 9-3 with 12:40 left in the first half. Three minutes later, after a 3-pointer by Guy and a trio of free throws by Hunter, U.Va.'s advantage had ballooned to 17-7 – its largest of the half.

Though both Hunter and Texas Tech's Jarrett Culver were 3 of 4 shooting from the free throw line in the first half, neither of the coveted NBA prospects was able to find his shooting touch early on.

Both players are projected by many draft analysts to be possible top-10 selections in the June draft if they leave school early. In addition to Hunter's first-half struggles, Culver missed all six of his shots in a half that saw them spend a lot of possessions guarding each other.

While Culver struggled to get rolling, Texas Tech discovered a massive spark from its perimeter shooting to get back in the game.

Scoring on five consecutive possessions, including four 3-pointers, Texas Tech knotted the game 21-21 with under 5½ minutes to go in the half. Francis had a pair of the 3-pointers for the Red Raiders.

The 3-point shooting barrage fueled a 12-2 run to put the Red Raiders up 25-21 with less than 4½ minutes remaining, but the four-point cushion would represent their largest lead of the half.

U.Va. regained momentum before halftime. After tying the game 29-29 on a turnaround jumper by Hunter with 1:30 left, Jerome capped the half with 1.5 seconds left by hitting a 3-pointer from the top of the key, pushing the Cavaliers into a 32-29 lead.

Standing on the floor after the game in the bedlam of U.Va.'s most satisfying men's basketball celebration on record, Jerome basked in a moment he'd waited all his life to experience.

"Forget last year," Jerome said. "This is everything you dream of since you're a little kid. I'm not even thinking about UMBC right now. I'm just thinking this is a dream come true, and it's even more than that because you never even imagine you'll be able to spend a year with people you actually love." ∎

Tony Bennett acknowledges the crowd before cutting down the net following U.Va.'s incredible championship performance. (Photo by Jonathon Gruenke)

Virginia 63, Auburn 62
April 6, 2019 • Minneapolis, Minnesota

HEART-STOPPER

Guy's late free throws cap Virginia's thrilling semifinal win

By Norm Wood

Last weekend, Mamadi Diakite made the biggest shot in Virginia men's basketball history with a game-tying 12-foot jumper at the end of regulation, knotting U.Va.'s eventual Elite Eight victory against Purdue.

Move over, Mamadi. There's a new greatest shot ever in U.Va. lore, and it belongs to Kyle Guy from the free-throw line Saturday night in the Cavaliers' 63-62 win against Auburn in the Final Four.

With U.Va. (34-3) trailing 62-60 in a national semifinal, Guy was fouled by Samir Doughty as the clock hit zero on a 3-point attempt from deep in the left corner.

After a review by officials resulted in six-tenths of a second being added to the clock, Guy proceeded to knock down two free throws to tie the game. Auburn called a timeout, just before Guy made the final free throw to seal the win.

"These are moments that every basketball player has dreamed of, hitting the game-winning shot or free throws or whatever," said Guy, who entered the game as a team-best 81.8 percent free-throw shooter on the season.

"Kind of had that feeling in your stomach, like a good nervousness, like, 'All right, this is my chance.' To be able to go to the national championship off of that for these guys and (U.Va.) coach (Tony) Bennett, I mean, I really don't have the words."

Auburn's desperation shot at the buzzer fell short.

U.Va. moves on to Monday night's championship game, where it will play Texas Tech, a 61-51 winner Saturday night against Michigan State in the other semifinal. It'll be the first appearances in the title game for both teams and will feature a matchup of two of the nation's top three scoring defenses (U.Va. is first, Texas Tech is third).

Before Guy got the ball for his attempted 3 on U.Va.'s final possession, Cavaliers guard Ty Jerome appeared to double-dribble after recovering a loose ball near midcourt on the heels of losing it off his foot, but the violation wasn't called.

Replays confirmed Jerome's double-dribble, but he had a different take on it after the game. He said officials let a lot of fouls slide in the game, including what he deemed a foul on Auburn's Bryce Brown on the play in the question, explaining in Jerome's opinion why officials didn't subsequently call him for a double-dribble.

Auburn coach Bruce Pearl was as diplomatic as possible about Jerome not getting whistled.

"We were in a situation late where we had some fouls to give, and I knew there was a disruption there," Pearl said. "You've just got to get on to the next play."

Enduring a full range of emotions down the stretch, U.Va. went from in control of the game to down in the waning seconds to the miracle finish.

"You know, we were 6 of 12 from the (free-throw)

With the season on the line, Kyle Guy shoots a free throw during the final seconds of Virginia's Final Four game against Auburn. (Photo by Jonathon Gruenke)

line," said U.Va. coach Tony Bennett, whose team went on to beat Purdue 80-75 in overtime in the Elite Eight after Diakite's shot at the buzzer in regulation tied it 70-70.

"For (Guy) in that (Final Four) setting to do it, yeah, it doesn't get much better than that."

With U.Va. trailing 61-57, Guy kept the Cavaliers in it on a 3-pointer with nine seconds left. It was just his second successful 3 of the game on six attempts.

Auburn's Jared Harper was fouled by Kihei Clark with seven seconds left and made 1 of 2 free throws. Harper's miss was rebounded by Jerome.

The Tigers, who had two fouls to give, committed a pair of fouls in the next five seconds before U.Va.'s final possession, which was punctuated by Doughty's foul on Guy and his decisive free throws. Guy finished with 15 points.

"I didn't want to have anything to do with my teammates or coaches at that time," Guy said of his mindset prior to stepping to the free-throw line. "I just wanted to be in my own space. I knew they had confidence in me. I just needed to build up my own."

Opposite: Kyle Guy and Ty Jerome celebrate taking a lead late in second half at U.S. Bank Stadium. Above: U.Va. fans watch the thrilling conclusion of the Cavaliers' 63-62 semifinal win. (Photos by Jonathon Gruenke)

Pearl argued to no avail against the foul called on Doughty, a VCU transfer who posted a team-high 13 points off the bench and paced Auburn's 23-2 advantage in bench points. Officials didn't review the foul called on Doughty, because fouls can't be reviewed via video replay.

As frenetic as the final seconds were for both teams, it was fitting considering the tenor of the closing minutes.

Clark and Jerome made 3-pointers on back-to-back possessions to put U.Va. up 50-43 with less than 8:40 left. Jerome, who led all scorers with 21 points, connected on another 3-pointer with 5:22 remaining to extend U.Va.'s lead to 57-47 — its largest of the game.

U.Va., which shot 49 percent from field, would fail on its next six shots from the floor as Auburn (30-10) went on a 14-0 run.

Despite missing 20 of its first 26 shots from 3-point range, Auburn still had some fight left down the stretch.

Opposite: Kyle Guy drives to the basket against Auburn's J'Von McCormick. Above: U.Va's Kihei Clark waits as his teammate Kyle Guy attempts the crucial free throws which would send Virginia to the NCAA tournament final. (Photos by Jonathon Gruenke)

Brown was unsuccessful on seven of his first eight attempts from long range, but it didn't affect him in the closing minutes.

Seconds after Jerome committed his fourth foul, Brown hit a 3-pointer with 4:24 remaining, trimming U.Va.'s lead 57-51. Another Brown 3 with 3:29 left cut U.Va.'s advantage to 57-54.

Daniel Purifoy reduced U.Va.'s lead to 57-56 on a jumper with 2:46 remaining before Brown hit his biggest shot of the game — yet another 3 to put Auburn up 59-57 as the clock rolled under two minutes.

Anfernee McLemore made a pair of free throws with 17 seconds left to give Auburn a 61-57 lead, but it wasn't enough. Auburn shot 38.2 percent from the floor for the game and 29 percent from 3-point range (9 of 31).

Leading 31-28 at halftime, Auburn had momentum going into the locker room.

Coming into the evening, U.Va. had surrendered an average of 18 points in the paint per game in the tournament. Auburn had already equaled that mark by halftime, but it had just four points in the paint in the second half.

Jerome was U.Va.'s only starter to shoot better than 33.3 percent from the floor before halftime. He made 5 of 9 field-goal attempts in the first 20 minutes, finishing the half with a game-high 13 points.

Auburn entered the game shooting 40.5 percent from 3-point range, but it was the Tigers' ability to penetrate the Cavaliers' pack-line defense that helped them regain the lead before halftime.

After U.Va. built an 18-13 cushion, Auburn scored 10 of its final 18 points in the half on layups and dunks. Though Auburn was just 3 of 14 from beyond the 3-point line in the first half, McLemore's 3 with 40 seconds remaining gave the Tigers their three-point halftime edge.

"Every round, I say the same thing almost," Jerome said of U.Va.'s run through the tournament this season after losing last year in the first round to No. 16 seed Maryland-Baltimore County. "It feels a little bit sweeter, a little bit sweeter. … It's an unreal feeling. We're going to do everything we can to finish the job." ∎

Tony Bennett shouts instructions to his players during the national semifinal game. (Photo by Jonathon Gruenke)

"These are moments that every basketball player has dreamed of," Kyle Guy said of the opportunity to shoot the game-deciding free throws for a spot in the tournament final. (Photo by Jonathon Gruenke)

INSPIRED AND HUMBLED

Bennett driven to coach U. Va. to a Final Four

By David Teel • November 2, 2018

After his team's crushing NCAA tournament defeat in March, Virginia basketball coach Tony Bennett heard from his friend Joe Stewart, a high school coach in Ohio. Offering reassurance, Stewart forwarded a copy of a letter Indiana's Bob Knight received in 1975.

Knight's squad had just completed a 31-1 season, its lone setback by two points to Kentucky in the NCAA Mideast Regional final. The letter's author was Hall of Fame coach Clair Bee.

"Take a deep breath, get your bearings, set your sights on even greater heights and start all over again," Bee began. "All a frustrated young man can expect to see as he looks over his shoulder is a desolate cemetery where his broken dreams lie buried in defeat."

Bee told the Hoosiers that a leader "is strengthened by the blow that cut him down. Now he knows the rough spots that pit the road and the quicksand that lies so innocently nearby. He knows because he has fought his way up that path of agony — almost to the very top."

Bee closed the four-paragraph letter — Bennett graciously sent me a copy — with a final portrayal of a leader: "He grasps the new challenge with eager hands, races for the starting line. He will be back!"

Bennett read Bee's letter to his team and believes the Cavaliers "could be terrific this year," if they heed its advice.

Shared at Atlantic Coast Conference media day, Bennett's anecdote did not mention the postscript:

Indiana went 32-0 the following season and remains men's Division I basketball's last undefeated national champion.

Not to suggest that Virginia will be the next. But similar to Knight's Hoosiers, Bennett's Cavaliers are certainly capable of rebounding from March's wrenching first-round tournament loss to Maryland-Baltimore County, reaching their third Final Four and winning the program's first national title.

U.Va.'s talent is that good. With veterans Ty Jerome, Kyle Guy, De'Andre Hunter, Jack Salt and Mamadi Diakite joining with newcomers Braxton Key and Kihei Clark, Virginia is No. 5 in the Associated Press preseason poll.

And Bennett, a three-time national Coach of the Year, is that driven. He is grounded by faith, inspired by success and humbled by failure, an exceptional blend.

Few have experienced such peaks and valleys in the same season.

The Cavaliers went an unprecedented 20-1 versus ACC rivals, sweeping the conference regular-season and tournament championships; they ascended to No. 1 in the polls and entered the NCAA tournament 31-2 and favored to reach their first Final Four since 1984.

But that quest ended abruptly March 16 as UMBC became the first No. 16 NCAA tournament seed to defeat a No. 1 seed, routing Virginia 74-54.

"It kind of sparked something in me," Bennett said. "I desperately want Virginia and this team that I

Tony Bennett has led Virginia to the NCAA tournament seven times in 10 seasons.

coach to have a chance to one day play for a national championship, to win a national championship, go to the Final Four. That has inspired me in a way maybe only a loss like that can.

"And that's important that I have that. But it did something else that I think's as important, or more important: It made me realize if that doesn't happen, I'm still OK. That's almost freed me up to go after my coaching this season and with this team in a better way and the right way."

Bennett won't suddenly adopt Bob Huggins' sideline antics at West Virginia. Indeed, his players and staff say outsiders may not even notice any changes.

But there are changes.

"He'll watch more film, or he'll have extra meetings with me about what I think about this offensive set or how can we add this to our game?" point guard Ty Jerome said.

"I don't think his personality or demeanor is going to change," associate head coach Jason Williford said. "I think it's just more attention to detail, some changes maybe X-and-O wise — I can't give away all our secrets — but just certain things we may have to do when we're struggling in certain areas, specifically offense."

This is Bennett's 13th season as a head coach: three at Washington State, with No. 10 at Virginia on the horizon. He's steered eight teams to the NCAA tournament and reached an Elite Eight and two other Sweet 16s. The Final Four has been elusive.

But major college basketball teems with coaches who endured long waits before making the national semifinals.

Jim Boeheim reached his first Final Four in his 11th season at Syracuse. Bo Ryan guided Wisconsin to 13 consecutive NCAA tournaments before crashing the Final Four in his 14th year. Mark Few's first Final Four came in his 18th straight tournament appearance with Gonzaga. Hall of Famer John Chaney coached Temple to 17 NCAA bids and never reached a national semifinal.

Tony Bennett's Virginia team rebounded from its stunning first-round loss to UMBC in the 2018 NCAA tournament, once again earning a No. 1 seed and advancing to the 2019 Final Four.

"I look at things differently now, actually better, from what I've experienced," Bennett said. "I think if you know you can handle … the worst thing that can happen and still find joy in the game, at some point you realize, 'Yeah, it stings, but it's OK and I made it through it.' I think that's worth everything, and I think it does allow you to go after it harder. …

"It was unbelievable to win like we won, and it was joyful. But it wasn't the end-all, be-all. And it was really painful to lose like we did, really painful, humbling. But it wasn't the end-all, be-all."

As always, Bennett's life perspective is rooted in his Christian beliefs. He doesn't volunteer this unsolicited, but whenever asked, he beams, even when it's related to adversity.

The challenge for each of us, Bennett said, is to discover our "secret of contentment." If it's only winning, the inevitable losing "will destroy you."

Bennett finds his contentment in his relationships with his wife, Laurel, their two children, and his players.

"That's unconditional," Bennett said, "and ultimately, that's based on my faith, and that's everybody's own individual journey. … This is all temporary, I understand that. This is fleeting. It's worth pursuing in the right way, and that's good. But if you don't have something else where you find your contentment away from the game … you're going to be torn up inside. I know that and I've experienced that."

Bennett's father, Dick, coached nine seasons at Wisconsin-Stevens Point and 10 at Green Bay before landing a marquee job at Wisconsin. In his fifth year with the Badgers, they reached the 2000 Final Four.

The milestone, Dick Bennett said at the time, doesn't compare with faith and family, and Tony Bennett can still recite the quote: "Because I know what truly matters, it enabled me to enjoy what seems to matter like this."

Tony Bennett smiles at the retelling.

"I'm a boring person," he said, "but I can talk about two things forever: basketball and faith. Because that's my joy." ■

During a season in which three ACC teams earned No. 1 seeds in the NCAA tournament, Virginia finished 16-2 in ACC play in 2019 to capture a share of the regular-season conference title.

Virginia 76, Maryland 71
November 28, 2018 • College Park, Maryland

ROAD WARRIORS

Exceptional poise carries U. Va. to win at Maryland

By David Teel

There is much to applaud about Virginia's 76-71 basketball victory at Maryland on Wednesday. Indeed, Jack Salt's career night, Kyle Guy's heat-check first half and another Ty Jerome dagger might well make U.Va.'s year-end highlight reel.

This will not, but this was central: In their first road test, against a ranked opponent defending aggressively, the Cavaliers committed two turnovers — both on offensive fouls.

Ponder that for a moment. No one dragged his pivot foot or threw a pass into the second row. No one fumbled a pass out of bounds or stepped on the baseline.

No one!

Not when the No. 24 Terps played man-to-man in the half court. And not when, trailing by double digits midway through the second half, they began pressing full-court.

At times deploying a five-guard lineup of Guy, Jerome, Braxton Key, De'Andre Hunter and Kihei Clark, fourth-ranked Virginia was impervious to the press. Moreover, the Cavaliers (7-0 for the third consecutive season) wisely attacked it, Hunter's transition dunk with less than two minutes remaining the punctuation.

"We took care of the ball," Virginia coach Tony Bennett said. "I don't want to minimize that because they can get out and run, and our ability … not to give them any loose-ball or live-ball turnovers was a big story."

Even for a program among the top 20 in ball security for a fifth straight year, Wednesday was a big deal.

To wit: The Cavaliers' turnover percentage of 11.7 this season ranks second among 353 Division I teams. Against Maryland, their percentage was 3.3. Moreover, the two turnovers matched a program low set in 2015 against Louisville.

"We have more people who can bring the ball up the floor (than last season)," Guy said. "Braxton has experience with the ball in his hands, and Kihei's tremendous at it. It's a (testament) to how we practice. We work on ballhandling and ball security every single day for at least 10 minutes."

Key's experience was at Alabama, where he played two seasons before transferring. Clark is a 5-foot-9 freshman point guard whom Bennett moved into a starter's role last Friday against then-No. 24 Wisconsin in the Battle 4 Atlantis championship game.

In 72 minutes of playing time since, Clark has no turnovers. Neither game was at home, and both were against top-25 opponents.

Granted, Wisconsin was more than content to play the deliberate pace Virginia prefers. Conversely,

De'Andre Hunter goes in for a layup during Virginia's win at Maryland in an ACC-Big Ten Challenge matchup. Hunter scored 15 against the Terrapins.

Maryland (6-1) wanted to create tempo, and a sellout crowd of 17,950 gathered for the ACC-Big Ten Challenge clamored for it.

To no avail. The Cavaliers' only turnovers were offensive fouls on Jerome and Mamadi Diakite.

Such composure figures to help Virginia against a schedule that includes impending road tests at South Carolina, Clemson, Duke, North Carolina, Virginia Tech and Syracuse.

The Cavaliers' ball security and quality offense helped them survive the Terps' 54-percent shooting and a combined 57 points from center Bruno Fernando and wings Anthony Cowan, Eric Ayala and Aaron Wiggins.

Virginia's points came from some usual suspects as Guy, Jerome and Hunter teamed for 50. Guy scored 15 of his game-high 18 in the first half, and Jerome, freed by a Salt screen, hit a clutch 3-pointer to bump the Cavaliers' lead to 66-59.

The outlier was Salt, the 6-foot-10, 250-pound redshirt senior from New Zealand. He scored a career-high 12 points, grabbed seven rebounds and played solid second-half defense on Fernando, who scored only four points after intermission.

Salt had yet to dunk in a game this season, and teammates were hazing him about it. Wednesday he dunked four times, all in the second half, two following offensive rebounds.

"He's the most selfless person on the team," Guy said. "He doesn't care about his touches. Today, so many people were attached to me, Dre and Ty when we drove. So, when Bruno went to block shots, Jack was there to put it in."

Salt's only other double-figure scoring games were 10-point efforts against Savannah State and East Carolina. Needless to say, Wednesday's outburst was more impressive — and critical.

So was his second-half checking of the springy, 6-10 Fernando, a future NBA draft choice. This came on the heels of Salt's credible defending of Wisconsin's Ethan Happ.

"Both great bigs," Salt said, "and traditional back-to-the-basket bigs. You don't see that very often today. I take that as a challenge. Just try to stay disciplined, stay physical and not give them anything easy on the rim."

Too often foul-prone, Salt committed only three Wednesday, which allowed him to play 33 minutes, the second-most of his career.

"Just doing my role," he said. "I know what I do. I gotta rebound, defend, stay out of foul trouble."

With Salt, juniors Guy, Jerome and Key, and precocious underclassmen in Hunter and Clark, all of Virginia's top six players understand their roles instinctively.

"Leadership and experience are what gets you through these games," said Key, who while with Alabama played in road games against the likes of Arizona, Kentucky, Florida, Texas, Oregon and Tennessee. "Having guys who have been here and done that helps. You can't really simulate that in any practice or any scrimmage, but when you get in the moment and you have a crowd of 16,000 cheering against you, it gets a little difficult." ■

Kihei Clark goes high in the air in the second half defending Maryland Terrapins guard Anthony Cowan Jr. Clark helped limit Cowan to 15 points on 5-of-12 shooting from the floor.

Virginia 65, Florida State 52
January 5, 2019 • Charlottesville, Virginia

KEY TO VICTORY

U. Va. puts away FSU behind shooting of Guy and Key, big defensive effort

By Norm Wood

With less than nine minutes left Saturday against Florida State, Virginia was enduring a stretch where it had misfired on 12 of 14 field-goal attempts, and De'Andre Hunter and Ty Jerome were a combined 4-of-19 shooting for the afternoon.

Bad news for U.Va. against the No. 9-ranked team in the nation, right? Not with the Cavaliers squeezing the life out of FSU's shooters and getting timely offensive boosts from Kyle Guy and Braxton Key.

Despite the rough patch in the second half, No. 4 U.Va. still maintained a 21-point lead before ultimately cruising to a 65-52 victory, its 11th straight in an Atlantic Coast Conference opener. Hunter and Jerome struggled, but Guy was as deadly shooting the ball in the first half as he's been all season.

"It was just going to be who could impose their will on each other and outlast," U.Va. coach Tony Bennett said regarding the mindset against FSU, which defeated the Cavaliers two seasons ago in John Paul Jones Arena and lost by four points last season to the Cavaliers in Tallahassee, Fla. "It's always been like that against (FSU coach Leonard Hamilton's) teams."

Guy had 21 points on 7-of-11 shooting from the floor, including 5-of-6 from 3-point range. Though quiet in the second half, Guy had 18 points in the opening 20 minutes and made all four of his 3-pointers.

"He's been shooting well in practice," Bennett said. "He's working at it. … I think he is mechanically sound, but what he has the ability to do is sometimes twist or turn in the air and find it. He can get it rolling, for sure, and we needed that."

From early in Monday's win against Marshall through the end of Saturday's first half, Guy connected on a school-record 11 consecutive 3-pointers. U.Va.'s previous record for consecutive 3-pointers made was eight, held by four players.

"You watch him play on film, and you just don't believe a guy is capable of being that confident," said Hamilton, whose team was led by Phil Cofer's nine points. "I'm not really sure I've seen many guys who seem to feel as good wherever he is on the floor that he's capable of putting it in the basket, and he does."

Guy couldn't recall — even during his high school days in Indianapolis — making as many as 11 straight 3-pointers in games.

"My freshman year (at U.Va.) I had a 16-0 run by myself, but that wasn't all field goals," said Guy, who scored a career-high 30 points against Marshall.

"When you hit a couple (3-pointers) in a row, Coach

Kyle Guy draws a foul as he goes up for a shot against Florida State. Guy led Virginia with 21 points on 7-of-11 shooting.

Bennett starts to run a couple plays for you, and that really helps."

Key had his most impactful game in a U.Va. uniform. He contributed 20 points on 7-of-11 shooting from the field to go along with six rebounds off the bench.

His 12 points in the opening half helped U.Va. (13-0, 1-0 ACC) overcome the poor shooting of Hunter and Jerome, who scored six points each in the game. For the first time all season, U.Va. didn't get a successful 3-pointer in a game from either Hunter or Jerome, who missed a combined five 3-point attempts (four by Jerome).

"Whenever I had an open look, I tried to be more aggressive (Saturday)," said Key, a transfer from Alabama whose previous high for U.Va. was 13 points in November against Middle Tennessee State.

As dazzling as Guy was early on against FSU (12-2, 0-1), U.Va.'s defense represented the biggest difference-maker. U.Va. held FSU to a season-worst 34 percent field-goal shooting.

U.Va., which shot 40.4 percent from the field (only 32 percent in the second half), made FSU pay for its transgressions, posting a 21-10 advantage in points off turnovers (11-0 in the first half). FSU committed 15 turnovers, while U.Va. had 11.

Leading 27-21 with less than 4½ minutes left in the first half, U.Va. went on a 15-2 run to close the half. FSU missed 10 of 13 shots in the final 16 minutes, 10 seconds of the half.

Key scored seven points during the run, including a pair of 3-pointers. U.Va.'s lead ballooned to 29 points in the second half.

"At the end, (FSU) might have scored a few off of our turnovers, but I think we were active," Bennett said.

"At times when we're playing, we have some versatility sizewise. … We clogged up some lanes, we showed on ball screens and got back quick." ∎

Jack Salt puts up a shot around an outstretched Seminoles defender.

HEAD COACH

TONY BENNETT

Tony Bennett followed providential path to U.Va.

By David Teel • March 13, 2018

The University of Virginia introduced Tony Bennett as its basketball coach the week of the 2009 Final Four. Inspired and clandestine, the search lasted 14 days.

But the journey that brought Bennett to Charlottesville began at least 17 years earlier with an obscure, fifth-round NFL draft choice by his beloved Green Bay Packers.

There were random meetings at Seattle Pacific, Colorado State and Portland State. There were diversionary tactics, considerable prayers and a telling endorsement from a complete stranger.

There were days of indecision, delayed phone calls and immeasurable anxiety. There was a matchmaker with better intuition than eharmony.com, and even a late-night pizza from Charlottesville's College Inn.

Why, this passage is so meandering and improbable as to be preordained.

"It certainly feels that way to us, for sure," says Bennett's wife of 22 years, Laurel.

With Virginia and Bennett the toast of college basketball and among the favorites to reach the Final Four, principals agreed for the first time to reveal details of how the search unfolded.

"It was," Liberty University coach and Bennett confidant Ritchie McKay says with a laugh, "an interesting process, and it's worked out. I'm happy for

U.Va., but even happier for Tony because I know he loves it there. What a marvelous job they've done."

Now about the NFL draft pick that started it all.

'Twas the basketball offseason of 1992, and Bennett was preparing for his own draft, the NBA variety. He had just completed an All-America career at Wisconsin-Green Bay, his hometown school and where he played for his father, Dick.

Five hours south, in Peoria, Ill., McKay was a fledgling assistant coach at Bradley University, assigned by his boss, Jim Molinari, to study tape of Dick Bennett's renowned defensive tactics. McKay was captivated, and when the Packers drafted his brother, University of Washington receiver Orlando McKay, he sensed an opportunity.

He called Dick Bennett and asked for an audience. Request granted.

Dick Bennett became McKay's mentor, and Tony Bennett became his dear friend.

Four years later, in 1996, McKay landed his first head-coaching position, at Portland State. The athletic director who hired him was Jim Sterk — the two had met years earlier at Seattle Pacific, where McKay was an assistant coach and Sterk an associate AD.

McKay and Sterk forged a lifelong friendship and an essential link in Bennett's path to Virginia.

Introduced as Virginia's coach in 2009, Tony Bennett has brought the basketball program back to prominence, culminating with a national championship in 2019. (Photo by Jonathon Gruenke)

"HE SAID HE WOULD NEVER BE A COACH"

By the time McKay went to Portland State, Bennett's NBA career was finished. The Charlotte Hornets had drafted him in the second round, but recurring foot injuries limited his effectiveness. He was toiling for New Zealand's North Harbour Vikings, who would eventually make him a player-coach.

Introduced by their pastor in Charlotte, David Chadwick, the Bennetts were newlyweds when they ventured to New Zealand. But coaching was not part of the plan. Tony was playing, while Laurel served as a youth pastor.

"I signed on when he said he would never be a coach," Laurel Bennett says. "He said, 'I've seen that life and what it does to my dad. It's crazy.' I said, 'Good, because that doesn't seem like a real good idea to me, either.' "

But McKay and others were convinced Bennett was made for coaching, and they beamed in 1999 as he returned from New Zealand and joined his dad's staff at the University of Wisconsin. In their first season coaching together, father and son helped the Badgers, a program with minimal basketball heritage, reach the 2000 Final Four.

Tony Bennett was hooked. So was Laurel. Coaching was their calling.

Three games into the 2000-01 season, citing burnout, 57-year-old Dick Bennett resigned as Wisconsin's coach. Tony Bennett remained on the staff as co-worker and friend Brad Soderberg guided the Badgers back to the NCAA tournament.

Wisconsin hired Bo Ryan as its full-time head coach in the spring of 2001, and he retained Bennett as an assistant. There Bennett remained until McKay called his friend Sterk two years later.

Sterk had since become Washington State's athletic director, and McKay was the University of New Mexico's head coach. Reeling from seven consecutive losing seasons, Washington State was searching for a new big whistle, and McKay had an idea.

Hire Dick Bennett and designate Tony Bennett as his successor. Soon thereafter, Sterk flew to Wisconsin and met with the Bennetts.

Sterk was sold but offered no guarantees of succession.

"No promises, no prenuptial going in that Tony was going to be the guy," says Sterk, now Missouri's athletic director. "But after a couple years I went to my president and said, 'We need to … give assurances that he's going to be the guy when Dick retires because if we don't, some Big Ten school's going to hire him out from under us.'

"I took some heat for doing it, but then Tony proved me right."

And then some.

Located in remote Pullman near the Idaho border, Washington State is among major college basketball's most imposing challenges. Facilities are sparse, resources limited and there's no natural recruiting base.

When Tony Bennett took over, the Cougars had earned four NCAA tournament bids in their history. Their only conference championship, regular-season or tournament, was in 1941.

Yet as a rookie college head coach in 2006-07, Bennett steered the Cougars to a 26-8 record, a second-place Pacific 10 finish and the second round of the NCAA tournament, the first time they'd advanced in the bracket since 1983. He was the consensus National Coach of the Year.

The next season, Washington State advanced to an NCAA regional semifinal for the first time since its 1941 squad lost the national championship game to Wisconsin. Never before had the Cougars competed in consecutive NCAA tournaments.

Bennett was winning just as his father had at Wisconsin, with a pack-line defense that clogs the interior and a patient offense that waits for the best shot, both of which slow games and frustrate opponents. Schools with far more basketball pedigree noticed.

"I WAS AMAZED"

Iowa, Indiana, Michigan and Marquette approached Bennett about their vacancies. He spoke directly with Indiana only, but the conversation was brief.

"It's a small world," Bennett says, "and we had had enough success … at Washington State. There were some other jobs that were high-profile that I wasn't interested in."

On March 12, 2009, Virginia lost to Boston College in the opening round of the Atlantic Coast Conference tournament to complete a 10-18 season. The record was the Cavaliers' worst in 41 years, and four days later, the university parted ways with fourth-year coach Dave Leitao.

Virginia had shared the ACC regular-season title in 2007 and reached the NCAA tournament's second round. But the Cavaliers were 9-25 versus their conference peers the following two years.

"It wasn't any one thing," says then-Virginia athletic director Craig Littlepage, who retired from the position last year. "It was just a view on my part that we hadn't made progress, and in fact that we were slipping. In Dave's first couple years I thought we were building, and then things started to erode."

Littlepage is a basketball lifer. He played at Penn. He coached at Villanova under Rollie Massimino and Virginia under Terry Holland. He served as head coach at Penn and Rutgers.

Littlepage's top lieutenant throughout his AD tenure was Jon Oliver, another basketball guy. Oliver played at Boise State, and before joining Littlepage's administrative staff at U.Va., he was an associate AD at Washington State.

Knowing that Virginia's most prominent basketball teams, during the 1980s under Holland and 1990s under Jeff Jones, were steeped in defense, Littlepage and Oliver developed a profile.

"You just can't take any really good basketball coach, put him at the University of Virginia and expect to be successful," Littlepage says. "It was going to be somebody that had a strong background defensively, that had a background in selecting kids that would be uniquely fitting at the University of Virginia from an academic standpoint and from a basketball standpoint as well. And someone that had a demonstrated history of being able to build programs at places that might not necessarily be top-10 programs."

Virginia wasn't top-10, but the Cavaliers played in 13 NCAA tournaments from 1981 to '97. Moreover, the program boasted one of the ACC's best venues in John Paul Jones Arena, which opened in 2006.

"Before you make a (coaching) change," Oliver says, "you're wondering if you have to make a change, what are you going to do? I'd spent time at Washington State, and I knew how they were challenged from a resource perspective, and I was amazed at what Dick and Tony were able to do to improve that program.

"And I remember staying up late at night watching their games and thinking, 'There's something about this guy.' And then talking to the people I knew from out there about what kind of person he was in the community, and I thought this guy would be perfect on a big stage like the ACC."

Bennett was among three on Virginia's immediate radar. Media at the time speculated on then-Minnesota coach Tubby Smith and then-Oklahoma coach Jeff Capel, but Littlepage and Oliver decline to confirm or deny.

"Weren't they trying to get Tubby Smith?" Bennett says. "You know how that stuff goes. I don't know how legit all that was. … Whether they had struck out on other guys, I don't know."

"This was definitely Jon's brainchild," Laurel Bennett says. "I don't think anyone besides Jon would have thought of Tony at Virginia."

THE MATCHMAKER STRIKES AGAIN

Littlepage served on the NCAA tournament selection committee from 2003 to '07, chairing the group during the 2005-06 season, and he mined those resources during this search. Among his first calls was to Tom Jernstedt, who as an NCAA executive oversaw the tournament from 1973 to 2011.

"He said to me, words of the effect, 'Craig, I have been around so many of these teams and so many of these coaches, and literally I've seen every one of the coaches that have been in the NCAA tournament for 30-some odd years, and the absolute best guy that I've seen in terms of working with his kids and getting the most out of his kids, and the guy I think would be the perfect fit for you, is the young guy at Washington State, Tony Bennett.'

"And he went on to say, 'Honestly, I don't know if you'll be able to get him. … He's turned down some pretty good places already. It doesn't look like he's somebody that's ready to move. But I'm telling you, he is the best.' "

Nine years later, Bennett is flattered and surprised to hear such praise.

"I don't know who that is," he says sheepishly and politely of Jernstedt.

Jernstedt has never met Bennett, but observations left a powerful impression.

"He appeared to be an outstanding individual," says Jernstedt, a 2017 Basketball Hall of Fame inductee, "and had all the coaching pedigrees. … He appeared to be a very bright, great defensive coach, but also knew the other side of the ball. Disciplined, very team-oriented. I just liked his style.

"Having sat at the official (scorer's) table of the NCAA tournament for 38 years, I had the opportunity to observe coaches up close. And I always had admiration for those coaches who conducted themselves in a positive way, those who were in control and were clearly coaching. One of my favorites was Dave Gavitt. He was a pretty good friend of mine. … Tony Bennett in my mind is cut from the same cloth as Dave Gavitt."

Gavitt coached Providence College from 1969 to '79, and his 1973 Friars, led by Ernie DiGregorio and Marvin Barnes, reached the Final Four. Gavitt later founded the Big East and in 2006 was inducted into the Basketball Hall of Fame.

Littlepage also sought Stan Morrison's counsel. A former University of Southern California head coach, Morrison served on the NCAA basketball committee with Littlepage, and Littlepage asked him to rank the Pac-10's coaches.

UCLA had reached three consecutive Final Fours under Ben Howland and was dominating the conference. Cal-Berkeley had hired Mike Montgomery, who had taken Stanford to the Final Four.

Morrison ranked Bennett No. 1.

Washington State's 2009 season ended with a National Invitation Tournament loss at Saint Mary's on March 13, the day after Virginia announced Leitao's departure. As Littlepage and Oliver vetted their three candidates, Bennett emerged, they say, as the clear choice.

But how to sell a coach who had already declined overtures from the likes of Indiana? The matchmaker knew.

Early during Oliver's time at Washington State, in the spring of 1999, the Cougars were searching for a basketball coach. Then-athletic director Rick Dickson sent Oliver to evaluate Colorado State's basketball coach.

Oliver purchased a ticket to the Rams' home NIT game, and after the contest, with minimal experience or discernment, he approached their coach on the floor, presented his business card and walked away. Oliver laughs at the memory.

The coach was Ritchie McKay.

Washington State hired Oklahoma State assistant Paul Graham instead, but unbeknownst to all, another bridge had been built along Bennett's path.

Virginia's search approaching its second week, Oliver pondered how to approach his No. 1 target.

"Here's what I did know from people out in Washington," Oliver says. "Tony was not about money. He's not going to go for the splashy presentation and hard-core recruiting pitch. He's a very loyal guy. He cared about the kids; he cared about the university. …

"I was sitting in my office at home thinking, OK, I've got to come up with a unique strategy to try and reach out to Tony to make sure it's impactful and he'll at least listen. I knew if I could get him to come into JPJ in a stealth way, where he could look at it and think about what's possible, without people asking him a bunch of questions about Virginia, and would you go there and all that, I knew if he could see himself operating on this stage with an asset to be able to recruit to. … So as I'm sitting there in my home trying to figure out what to do, I swear to you the phone rings."

It was McKay.

Led by freshman guard Seth Curry, McKay's Liberty team had just completed a 23-12 season, the highlight of which was a victory at Virginia. Oliver figured McKay wanted to pitch himself for the job.

"I'm thinking, I don't have time for this right now," Oliver says.

But McKay wasn't stumping for himself. He was suggesting Tony Bennett.

Oliver: "I said, 'Ritchie, you won't believe this. I'm sitting here right now trying to figure out how to approach Tony.' I said, 'Here's what I want you to do. I want you to hang up the phone, I want you to call Tony right now and ask him if he's willing to talk to us. He needs to ask (his athletic director) for permission. … But tomorrow morning I'll have a plane on the tarmac. We'll have him back the next day, and no one will ever know he's gone.' "

McKay called Bennett with Oliver's offer.

"I'm like, 'Whoa, whoa, whoa, wait a second, Ritchie,' " Bennett says.

But Bennett was intrigued. He considered Virginia the Stanford of the East, and after consulting with his dad, wife and McKay, decided to listen.

"I just, I don't know," Bennett says. "Something was right about Virginia, and that's when I contacted our AD."

Sterk was realistic.

"They had a new arena," he says, "they were in the ACC, and I thought he'd have the opportunity to succeed there. I understood that opportunity calling. I didn't encourage him, but I knew that was one he should take a look at."

PIZZA DELIVERY

No media outlets, none, had linked Bennett to Virginia, and Oliver wanted more of the same. Public speculation, he believed, would prompt Bennett to withdraw.

So rather than use Virginia's private jet, which reporters and/or fans could easily track, Oliver leased a jet to bring the Bennetts to Charlottesville. And to be sure, he asked the pilot to pick them up in Spokane, Wash., 80 miles north of Pullman, and to refuel in the Midwest — Oliver and the Bennetts recall it was somewhere in Iowa.

"We were like, man, this is crazy," Laurel Bennett says.

On March 24, at about 9 p.m., local time, the Bennetts landed in Charlottesville. Oliver greeted them and immediately drove them to John Paul Jones Arena.

They toured the complex, though the lights were dim. No need to risk attention.

"I made arrangements with the building manager,"

Oliver says. "I wanted everybody out. I wanted one or two people there. I wanted to know exactly who was in the building."

Oliver drove the Bennetts to the Boar's Head Inn a few minutes away, and from their suite the couple ordered pizza delivered from the College Inn.

"I remember thinking, hey, this pizza is pretty good," Tony Bennett says.

Other than Sterk and family friends who were watching the kids, the Bennetts told no one in Pullman they were flying to Charlottesville. But after scarfing the pizza, Tony called his top Washington State assistant, Ron Sanchez.

"He had not taken visits to any other places," Sanchez says. "This was different. Then he said to me, 'You should see this place.' "

The Bennetts saw even more the next day. After huddling in their suite with Oliver and Littlepage for about 90 minutes, they strolled U.Va.'s renowned Lawn and saw Jefferson's Rotunda.

They weren't in Pullman anymore.

But the Bennetts were confused. Why were students walking outside in bathrobes?

Oliver and Littlepage explained that rooms on the Lawn don't have showers and that students were headed to the bathhouse. Then, fearing that Tony Bennett would be recognized, they ushered the couple to lunch inside a pavilion.

"Craig and Jon, first of all, were really good at selling the school," Laurel Bennett says. "And then, we felt they were sincere, and it proved to be true, as far as, it was a big deal for us to feel like we trusted them, and it was a big deal for us to say, OK, are there realistic expectations? …

"You watch people at press conferences and things they say. 'We want to win national championships.' You want to be with people who see the world the right way, who are realistic. We felt that. We liked everything they had to say."

Per McKay's suggestion, Virginia included Laurel Bennett in all meetings, which she and her husband appreciated. They are a team, and a decision of this magnitude had to be made together.

Unnoticed by anyone in Charlottesville, the Bennetts flew home that evening, this time directly to Pullman. No formal offer had been extended, but the unspoken truth was the job was Bennett's for the taking.

"Here's how I knew we had him," Oliver says. "When we were done, (Laurel) actually gave me a hug."

Oliver had no idea that Laurel Bennett would rescue the search.

PRAYER AND INDECISION

Less than 48 hours after the Bennetts departed, Oliver and Bennett talked contract terms — Bennett retains Spokane attorney Brad Williams to review such documents but does not have an agent. This was Friday, March 27, and Oliver suggested Bennett take the weekend to decide.

Bennett said he would call back at 1:30 p.m., Eastern time Monday. Thus began three days of prayer, discussion and vacillation in Pullman.

"Getting back that day, that night, I said 'I think this is right,' " Bennett says. "I went to sleep, and the next day, all of a sudden, I have to tell these young men and the administration that I'm leaving. After that, obviously I had a meeting with the president there (Elson Floyd). …

"It was one of those situations where you start thinking about it, and I had a really good team coming back with Klay Thompson. I really liked that team, and that's such a hard thing. That's where I took another day and I told Laurel I think it's best that we just stay."

Bennett picked up the phone to call Littlepage and decline. His wife stopped him.

"I wasn't trying to persuade him," Laurel Bennett says. "I felt like we needed to pray about this. We had done all the pros and cons, all the traditional stuff that way, but we decided we were going to pray about it. And part of that prayer is always, 'Let us be on the same page.' We kept going back and forth; we kept changing our minds. …

"He did, he had the phone in his hand. He was ready to do it. (But) so many of the cons were the people we were leaving, who we loved, and the parents and the recruits. Those people are always going to be there. And I didn't want him to stay for reasons of things you don't

want to do. I wanted to make a decision based on going toward something, even if that meant staying. …

"And the main thing I said to him was, 'Don't call yet because I think you should feel the same way for 24 hours. If you had called last night, you would have taken it. We need to be on the same page, and we need to be on that page for at least 24 hours before we move on.' "

The Bennetts turned to the same page Monday, March 30. But the scheduled 1:30 p.m., call to Littlepage and Oliver was late.

Terminally stoic, Littlepage remained calm. Edgy and transparent, Oliver bounced off walls.

There was no Plan B. If Bennett declined, the search would restart from scratch.

At about 2 p.m., Bennett called. The Cavaliers had their next coach.

"We had a peace about it," Laurel Bennett says. "That's the only way I can explain it. … We've made a lot of decisions together. I feel like we've gotten good at trusting each other. I appreciate how he is in the process as far as really caring about my opinion."

Bennett met with Washington State's players that afternoon, and the school promptly announced his departure for Virginia. The following day, U.Va.'s private jet flew to Pullman to bring the Bennetts to their new home.

Though disappointed, a contingent of Cougars fans gathered at Pullman's airport to cheer Bennett and thank him for reviving the program, which hasn't returned to the NCAA tournament since.

On Wednesday, April 1, Virginia introduced Bennett at a news conference in John Paul Jones Arena.

"DO IT YOUR WAY"

As at Washington State, the on-court foundation of Bennett's U.Va. program is defense. Off the court, Bennett preaches five pillars: humility, servanthood, passion, unity and thankfulness, and the combination has elevated Virginia to new heights.

Virginia has won more games versus ACC rivals in the last five years than in the previous 11 combined, and last week the United States Basketball Writers Association named Bennett its National Coach of the

Year for the third time, the second while at Virginia.

"He's special," Oliver says. "Every single day I worked with that man, it was the easiest thing I ever knew. His questions, his thoughtfulness, how he was prepared. I would always answer, 'Tony, do it your way.' Because in the first year or two you could tell he was so spot-on with what he was doing.

"He just got it. … He knew what to ask. He knew when to ask for advice. It was just amazing, and then to watch Laurel standing right there with him every step of the way, it was just a blessing."

Sanchez was a staple of Bennett's Washington State staff and has remained so at Virginia. Yet even after a dozen seasons, he marvels.

"I never doubted he would be able to win," Sanchez says. "Like his father, it was just a matter of time. … I knew the blueprint was already there, and I'd seen him follow it so closely (at Washington State). … So I never doubted it was going to be good. Did I ever imagine it was going to be this good? It never crossed my mind.

"I'm just so thankful that I'm a part of, that I can witness this first-hand, as opposed to from a distance, because the inner workings are what truly make it special."

Bennett has a saying: "Give it your best and live with it." So while others stress over wins and losses, he commits to the process.

Sure, Bennett burns to join his father as a Final Four head coach and to cut down the nets after a national championship. But the fire does not engulf him.

Here is how Laurel Bennett describes her husband's outlook:

"This is what I do. I'll give it my best and I'll live with it. But the other side of that coin is who I am, which is more important than what I do. And I am a child of God, and my values come from something other than my job."

As Bennett's national profile has grown, so has demand for his services. College and NBA teams have inquired, but Bennett, 48, has not been interested.

Toward that end, Littlepage, Oliver and U.Va.'s administration were proactive in enhancing Bennett's contract and remaining attentive to the program's needs. That responsibility now rests with new athletic director Carla Williams and incoming university president James Ryan.

Oliver considers the NBA the greatest threat to Virginia retaining Bennett.

"I'm not going to say who it was or when or how many," he says, "but I've been faced with that already. I don't think that Tony feels that the time is right. I believe his thinking has evolved over time and that if this thing continues to grow as it has and he's happy, because remember, he's changing people's lives right now. It's not just basketball.

"You look at his former players, they're all doing some pretty special stuff. I think as he sees more and more of that, it will impact his thinking on the NBA. … He's one of the most competitive people I've ever seen, and the opportunity at the highest level is something that will probably always be there in the background. …

"I believe Tony Bennett can have an amazing, Hall of Fame career right here at the University of Virginia over time. … It would be amazing if he stayed right here."

Ritchie McKay agrees. Final Fours, national championships and the Hall of Fame are possible.

McKay left Liberty in 2009 and spent the next six seasons as Bennett's associate head coach at Virginia before returning to Liberty as head coach in 2015. Essential and covert, his role in bringing Bennett to Charlottesville may be the greatest assist in Cavaliers basketball history.

But he deflects credit and embraces the suggestion that a higher power has steered this journey for upward of 25 years.

"Amen," McKay says. ∎

Virginia 81, Virginia Tech 59
January 15, 2019 • Charlottesville, Virginia

EARLY AND OFTEN

U.Va. continues ACC dominance with rout of Hokies

By David Teel

Repeat after me, Virginia faithful. Say it slowly. Say it often.

It's early. It's January.

It's early. It's January.

Very good. Now take a deep breath and say it again. Done? Relaxed? Lose that giddiness yet?

It's not easy, is it? Not when your Cavaliers are playing as well as any college basketball team in America.

And this hasn't been some brief glimpse. Tuesday's 81-59 flogging of Virginia Tech at John Paul Jones Arena ran U.Va.'s record to 16-0, 4-0 in the ACC, and was its seventh consecutive victory by at least 13 points.

Care to guess how many games in which the No. 4 Cavaliers have trailed in the second half? One. Yes, one!

VCU actually led Virginia by five with less than seven minutes remaining before the Cavaliers surged to a 57-49 win.

That was a nonconference test, and surely the thorny ACC will further challenge Virginia, likely as soon as the next game at Duke. But to date, no league foe has extended the Cavaliers.

The Hokies (14-2, 3-1 ACC) arrived in Charlottesville ranked ninth nationally and riding a nine-game winning streak, but Virginia never trailed. The Cavaliers led by 22 points at halftime and by at least 14 for the final 25 minutes.

"We punched them in the mouth, and they fought back a little bit," Virginia guard Kyle Guy said, "and then we just kept our foot on the pedal."

As they've done against every ACC foe.

Virginia led Florida State by 19 at halftime and by 29 with 2:18 remaining before FSU closed with a 16-0 run against U.Va.'s walk-ons. The Cavaliers led at Boston College by 30 en route to a 27-point victory. Three days later at Clemson, they won by 20.

"The scores and all that are a little overrated," Virginia coach Tony Bennett said.

Fair enough. But it's not like the Cavaliers are inflating their margins with late free throws or 3-point flurries. They have just been superior in every way.

But again, it's only mid-January, and 14 ACC games remain, and while its defense is a near-constant, surely Virginia can't sustain this dominance. And that's not a knock at the Cavaliers. No college squad could continually boatrace the teams in this league.

With Guy, Ty Jerome, De'Andre Hunter, Braxton Key, Mamadi Diakite, Kihei Clark, Jack Salt and Jay Huff blending seamlessly, the obvious difference in Virginia is offense. The Cavaliers are shooting 49.8 percent overall and 46.3 percent from deep in league play and rank fourth nationally in offensive efficiency.

Led by Hunter's game-high 21 points and Jerome's 14 points and JPJ-record 12 assists, Virginia shot 58.3 percent Tuesday and made 13 of 24 3s in the first top-10 clash in this rivalry's history.

"Very rarely do they take a forced shot," Tech coach

Jay Huff throws it down in the win against rival Virginia Tech. Huff had seven points and two rebounds off the bench.

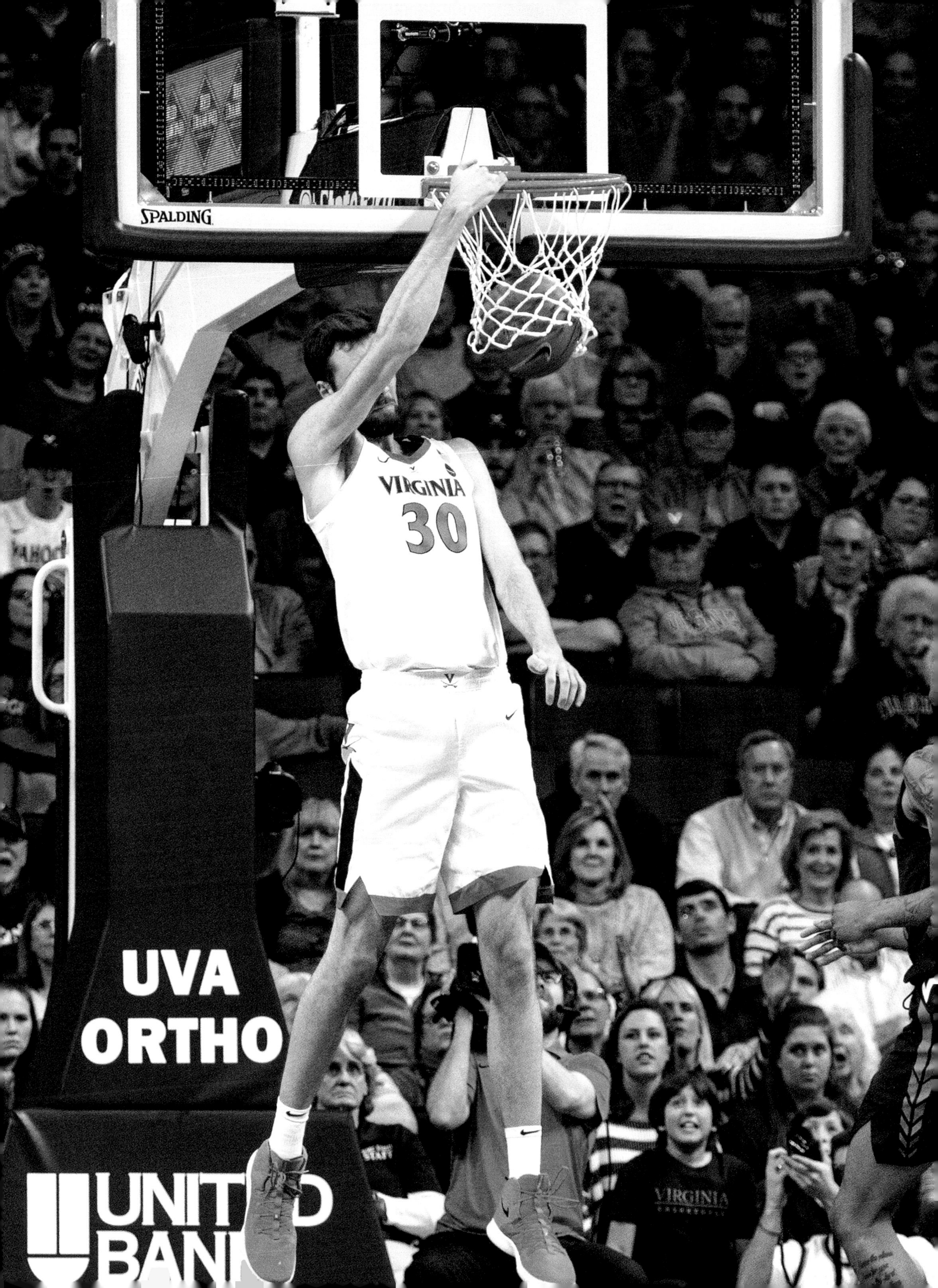
SPALDING
VIRGINIA
30
UVA
ORTHO
UNITED
BANK
VIRGINIA

Buzz Williams said. "They're very comfortable late in the (shot) clock. So I think that defensively you're stressed from the very beginning. ...

"We were just behind. Behind on ball pressure, behind on rotation, behind on stunts. And with space, categorically, their whole team can make shots and they did it for sure in the first half."

Flawless is a dangerous word, be the commodity gems or jumpers. But dang, Virginia's first half was close.

Creating open looks with superb passing, the Cavaliers made 10 of 14 from beyond the arc, with Jerome, Guy, Clark and Huff contributing. Clark's right-corner 3 at the first-half horn was the fitting conclusion and sent Virginia to intermission with a 44-22 lead.

Moreover, the Cavaliers committed only four turnovers in the opening half. 44 points on 26 possessions calculates to 1.67 points per possession, unthinkable against a Tech defense yielding 0.928 points per possession prior to Tuesday.

"Everybody shared the ball," Bennett said, "and you could tell they had fun playing together. And how could you not in this environment?"

This week is the first time since 2002 that Virginia is playing consecutive games versus top-10 opponents. And Saturday at No. 1 Duke, the Cavaliers will attempt to win back-to-back contests against the top 10 for the second time in program history.

The first was the 1976 ACC tournament semifinal and final over No. 9 Maryland and No. 4 North Carolina.

With point guard Tre Jones sidelined indefinitely with an injured right shoulder, the Blue Devils are wounded after Monday's overtime home loss to Syracuse — Duke had been 90-0 all-time as a No. 1 squad facing an unranked opponent, according to ESPN's crack research crew.

Still, bank on a supreme effort from the Blue Devils — and Cavaliers.

"The league will test you," Bennett said, "but obviously I like how we've withstood it so far."

Bennett knows.

It's early. It's January.

It's early. It's January. ∎

De'Andre Hunter drives to the hoop in the dominating win over the Hokies. Hunter had 21 points and five rebounds.

33

CENTER

JACK SALT

Salt uses grittiness to pave way to essential role

By Norm Wood • March 8, 2019

When Jack Salt arrived at Virginia in 2014 as a freshman from his native New Zealand, he did so as a member of his homeland's U20 national team — an honor he sure as heck didn't earn based solely on his defensive acumen.

Instead, Salt showed up in Charlottesville as a versatile big man who could score. Yes, the 6-foot-10, 250-pound center who has become No. 2 U.Va's most dependable low-post defender, a devastating screener and a guy who's regarded as one of the ACC's most imposing players by several of the conference's coaches was once an offensive weapon.

That was a lifetime ago.

Coming to play for U.Va. coach Tony Bennett, the nation's most dedicated defensive practitioner, Salt wasn't exactly sure what he was getting himself into in a Cavaliers uniform. As he prepares for Senior Day on Saturday against Louisville, it's clear he found his niche, serving as a three-year starter for U.Va. after wondering if he'd ever spend much time on the floor in America.

"I didn't know I was going to be a part of it," said Salt, who will be accompanied on the John Paul Jones Arena floor for Senior Day festivities by his father, Simon Salt, and mother, Maria Anstis, from New Zealand, and his sister, Sophia Salt, who is a 6-3 sophomore rower at Oklahoma. "I didn't have any expectations."

It's easy to get lost on a roster that during his time at U.Va. has featured Malcolm Brogdon, De'Andre Hunter, Kyle Guy and Ty Jerome, four players who certainly possess defensive chops but have been recognized as guys who score with regularity. Salt traded in the offense-first game when he left New Zealand, where he averaged 18.9 points and 14.8 rebounds per game for Westlake Boys High in Auckland.

Oh, but Salt's value isn't lost on those who've seen their guards run into a wall on occasion while being screened by Salt in games.

"The guy who doesn't get enough credit is Salt," Boston College coach Jim Christian said. "I just think he's such a good player at what he does, and when you do get chances to get by them, he's such a good guy at protecting the basket without fouling. To me, that's really what it's all about."

Big man Jack Salt is an anchor in the post on defense for U.Va.

Despite averaging only 3.8 points per game this season — his career high — while getting up just 2.7 shots per game, Salt remains an indispensable cog in U.Va.'s operation. Forward Mamadi Diakite, a redshirt junior, has often mentioned how working with Salt in practices and watching him in games has aided the development of his own defensive game.

Jerome, the beneficiary of dozens of Salt screens, appreciates the portions of Salt's game that don't show up in box scores.

"I think this year Jack has been an asset and has done something that not many people are asked to do," Jerome said. "He doesn't know going into a game how many minutes he's going to get, or if he's even going to take one shot during the game. His attitude never changes. He will give 110 percent for us every single possession, and that's something you don't see in almost any other guy in the country. If you ask them to play 30 minutes one game and five minutes the next, I don't know if any other guy in the country will give you their all, and he does."

LEARNING FROM HIS ELDERS

Salt's evolution as a defensive whiz didn't happen overnight. Seeking to identify his avenue to playing time during a redshirt year in the '14-15 season, Salt did what most U.Va. hoops newbs do when they're trying to learn the nuances of the pack-line defense. He mimicked the veterans.

"I looked at (Isaiah Wilkins) a lot and I looked at Darion (Atkins) and the way they defended," said Salt, who in 4½ years has an undergraduate degree in anthropology and is finishing his master's degree in U.Va.'s Curry School of Education. "When I came in as a freshman, (Atkins) was just an amazing defender. … Just me being motivated every day to get better at it, and just understanding it's hard and that you're not going to be good at it to start with and that you're going to be

bad at it, then listening to the coaches and observing other players, that's probably the best way I'd explain a big man trying to get better at the (pack-line) defense.

"It's just tough for any player when you come from scoring a lot in high school to college and you haven't got that same role. You've got to adjust if you want to play."

Atkins and Wilkins played with an edge for U.Va., guys with an attitude on the court who weren't afraid to take on the tough-guy persona. Partially by osmosis, and certainly by necessity, Salt latched on to that rough-as-sandpaper quality.

"When he's out there, he's got such a physical presence around the rim," Louisville coach Chris Mack said. "Nobody is going to push him off his spot or bully him for offensive rebounds. He's just strong. He's experienced. He moves his feet extremely well. So often in the game nowadays, big guys have to be able to deal with ball screens on the perimeter. The way Tony chooses to play those, your bigs are going to have to really move their feet. I think Jack does it as well as anybody in our league."

Having coached against Salt for three seasons prior to this year, Clemson's Brad Brownell already had a good feel for the kind of bruiser his players faced when the Tigers played the Cavaliers, but South Carolina coach Frank Martin provided further insight to Brownell. After Martin's Gamecocks lost 69-52 at home in December to the Cavaliers, Martin told Brownell that South Carolina forward Chris Silva, a 6-9 senior, had gotten his fill of Salt.

"That's one thing that Chris Silva said, was Jack Salt was the strongest guy he's played against at South Carolina," Brownell said. "Obviously, (Salt) can move, he can hedge ball screens, he can sprint up and down the floor, big and strong at the rim.

"We want Trey Jemison, one of our freshman post players, to grow up and be like Jack Salt. I think that would be fantastic."

Jack Salt was a more offensively focused player in high school in New Zealand but has embraced his role as a screener and defensive stalwart at Virginia.

"WHATEVER YOU ASK"

After playing professionally in 1996 and '97 for the North Harbour Vikings in Auckland, before coaching the Vikings in '98 and '99, Bennett is no stranger to Salt's ilk. Bennett recognizes Salt learned how to become a leader from Wilkins, who came to U.Va. in the '14 class along with Salt and whom Salt refers to as one of his best friends.

As for Salt's approach to the game, well, that wasn't necessarily a learned trait. It's in the blood, according to Bennett.

"If you know anything about the culture of New Zealand, Jack embodies that to the fullest extent," Bennett said. "He's just a hard-working, blue-collar guy. You watch the way he plays and how competitive he is. He's improved slowly through the years with some of his development, but his heart and his physicality — I know the game's (all about) freedom of movement and taking the physicality out of it — but you need physicality and he brings a level of physicality that's really important for us. … He's willing to do whatever you ask. He'll screen, he'll run the floor, he'll do all those kinds of things."

After starting 50 consecutive ACC games, Salt didn't start Feb. 27 against Georgia Tech because of a bad back. No chance it keeps him off the floor Saturday afternoon.

"It's a lot better," said Salt, who added he has British and New Zealand passports and plans to try to play in an international pro league. "I just needed a little rest. It just flared up during the season. It's hard to get prolonged rest when you've got at least one game every week, but it's doing really well. The strength and conditioning coaches have been doing a really good job. I'm feeling good. I'm ready to finish out the season strong." ■

Jack Salt has been the ultimate teammate in his five years at U.Va., always doing whatever was asked of him by Tony Bennett and the coaching staff.

Duke 72, Virginia 70
January 19, 2019 • Durham, North Carolina

DEVILS TAKE BATTLE OF THE TITANS

Duke topples U. Va. in postseason-caliber clash

By David Teel

College basketball's most interesting teams collided Saturday night at Cameron Indoor Stadium.

Are Duke and Virginia the best teams? We're months from answering that question, but the Blue Devils and Cavaliers did nothing to dispel the notion.

Duke 72, Virginia 70.

Stirring, exhausting, remarkable. You choose the adjective. Maybe all of the above, and then some.

Oh, neither team approached perfection. But that's what happens in a frenzied, overheated arena, where your muscles scream and breath vanishes and, oh, by the way, the other team has guys on scholarship, too.

You can parse any number of sequences or possessions to separate these two national contenders, but the difference was rooted in the Duke freshmen many expect to go 1-2 in this year's NBA draft.

Zion Williamson (27 points and nine rebounds) and RJ Barrett (30 points and five rebounds) played 78 of 80 possible minutes — Barrett never sat — and ravaged No. 4 Virginia (16-1, 4-1 ACC) like no teammates have in Tony Bennett's 10 seasons coaching the Cavaliers.

Indeed, the last time teammates had scored 25 or more against Virginia was November 2008, when Liberty's Seth Curry and Kyle Ohman had 26 apiece in a Flames victory.

"We're a solid defensive team," Bennett said, "but tonight we were not solid enough, large credit due to their play."

Correction: The Cavaliers are an exceptional defensive team. But Williamson and Barrett penetrated at will and combined to shoot 21 of 35 from the field.

"Wow, that's a high-level game," Duke coach Mike Krzyzewski said. "That's a big-time game. They don't get much better than that. The kids on both teams, every possession was good. If you scored, you beat good defense; if you didn't score, good defense beat you. Every possession was high-level."

Top-ranked Duke (15-2, 4-1) punished Virginia on the glass in the first half, grabbing nine offensive rebounds and scoring 11 second-chance points. In the second half, the Devils missed only seven shots, rendering offensive rebounds moot.

This Duke did with its engine, freshman point guard Tre Jones, sidelined with a right shoulder injury suffered in Monday's overtime loss to Syracuse. Without his team's best defender, Krzyzewski overhauled his defensive game plan and had his players switch every screen, even if that left 6-foot-11 Marques Bolden checking 5-9 Kihei Clark.

Led by De'Andre Hunter's 18 points, Virginia exploited that strategy for much of the evening, beating

Ty Jerome had 14 points, but it wasn't enough in Virginia's 72-70 loss to Duke.

defenders off the dribble. But the Cavaliers, who began the night as the ACC's No. 2 team in 3-point accuracy at 40.2 percent, missed 14 of their 17 attempts from beyond the arc.

But there was no discernible frustration from Bennett or his players afterward. Nor should there have been after a night in which one second-half stretch saw the lead flip on 12 consecutive scores.

This was a March- or April-caliber clash between two teams that have faced intense scrutiny since the season began in November.

That Virginia was Division I's last undefeated squad this year following last season's 31-3 finish was beyond impressive. The Cavaliers' first-round NCAA tournament demise to UMBC last March still doesn't compute, and their reaction to that historic disappointment was always going to be a prevailing story in 2018-19.

Almost anyone with a heart applauded the grace, perspective and eventual humor that Bennett and his players displayed in the immediate aftermath. But how would they respond this season between the lines?

Admirably, I would say.

Meanwhile, Duke, which saw four freshmen from last season's Elite Eight squad head to the NBA, assembled an even more gifted recruiting class. We can only imagine the hype Michigan's Fab Five of the early 1990s would have prompted in a social media age, but this year's Duke class was assured constant attention, if only because of Williamson.

His dunking has been an Internet rage for years, and his Instagram followers number more than 2.2 million, or about 245 times the capacity of Cameron Indoor Stadium.

But there's so much more than the dunking.

"That move he made in the open court and dunk with the right hand," Krzyzewski said of a play on which Williamson grabbed a rebound, crossed over Ty Jerome and dunked over 7-1 Jay Huff. "Holy mackerel."

Yeah, pretty much. The guy's handle and dexterity are stunning for a 285-pounder.

"An unusually great player," Krzyzewski said.

Williamson and Barrett were so good that Duke overcame Virginia's 52.8 percent shooting. When the Cavaliers shoot that well, they're usually unbeatable.

The last time the Cavaliers shot better than 50 percent and lost? Six years ago at North Carolina.

Virginia had won 59 consecutive games when making more than half its shots and was 83-2 in such contests under Bennett — the other setback was to Maryland in 2010.

"NBA team," Virginia's Kyle Guy said of Duke. "That's the only thing I can think of in terms of talent and size and length. We're probably not going to see another team like that. But I think we're just as versatile as them and just as talented. They just got the better of us tonight."

The Cavaliers won't see another team like this until Feb. 9 in Charlottesville, when the Blue Devils come calling for a rematch.

"They're terrific," Krzyzewski said, "and hopefully we bring the best out of each other. We'll have a hell of a game when we play them up there." ∎

Freshman phenom Zion Williamson lived up to his billing against U.Va., scoring 27 points and grabbing nine rebounds.

11
GUARD

TY JEROME

Ty Jerome's dad taught him the tough love of basketball since birth

By David Teel • March 27, 2019

Tony Bennett knows the perils of playing for your father. As a 1988 high school All-American in Green Bay, Wis., he accepted a scholarship from the local university, coached by Wisconsin basketball icon Dick Bennett.

"Everything is exaggerated," Tony Bennett said. "The good is great, and the bad is terrible, depending on what your father is like. … But you know it comes from love. That's the one thing I had to learn as a head coach, and my dad shared that with me.

"He said, 'Son, I pushed you hard. You gave me a green light.' I said, 'Push me. I want this team to go as far as it can and I want a chance to play after college. You've got a green light to do whatever you think it takes to make me and this team as good as you can to me.' I regretted saying that so many times, and he dangled me over the edge, but I always knew, 'This is my dad saying it.' It's almost like a safety net."

Preparing his Virginia Cavaliers for their third NCAA regional semifinal in the past six years — they encounter Oregon on Thursday in Louisville, Ky. — Bennett has compared notes with Ty Jerome, U.Va.'s All-ACC point guard. There's one XXL difference in their experiences: Bennett, the NCAA's career 3-point percentage leader and a 1992 second-draft choice by the NBA's Charlotte Hornets, chose to be coached by his father at Green Bay. Moreover, at age 19, he was more than old enough to understand that Dick Bennett's ruthless standards were rooted in love.

Jerome was far too young to grasp such a concept when his father decided to be his coach. And when, exactly, did Mark Jerome start coaching Ty?

"When he came home from the hospital," Mark said matter-of-factly. "I put a basketball in his crib, and everybody thought I was crazy. Doesn't mean I'm not still."

Indeed, Ty Jerome was born to basketball. His dad played college ball at Lafayette, and his mom, Melanie Walker, played at Brandeis.

Raised in Harlem, Mark Jerome learned basketball on New York City's unforgiving street courts. He gave his oldest son the same education, and Ty, a 6-foot-5 junior, developed into Virginia's most dependable clutch shooter and a projected first-round NBA draft pick.

But neither sugarcoats the tension their journey created.

They started with Ty sitting on Mark's lap watching

From the cradle to the championship: Ty Jerome's father, Mark, once placed a basketball in his infant son's crib, hoping to instill an early passion for the game.

games on TV in their uptown Manhattan home. Then came a portable hoop that hung on whatever fence was available, then, as a toddler, actual games.

"When you're playing street tournaments in New York City, there's lots of pressure," Mark said. "There's lots of fans and lots of people talking trash. … It's super-intense. There were times we were playing four boroughs in one day. … There were times we had so many games … (that) somebody should have called (social services) on me."

Not that Ty minded. To this day, competitive basketball is his nirvana.

But when the trash-talking comes from your dad, and when it's often aimed at you, well, that's not quite so blissful. Mark's yelling was so incessant that Ty became immune.

He certainly didn't like it, and he occasionally fired back. But age and maturity taught him to filter out the noise and absorb the lessons.

"No coach is ever going to be harder on me than my dad was when he coached me," Ty said, "no matter what level. … I have a million stories to prove that."

I asked him to share one or 10. He smiled and declined.

"Looking back on it and the mistakes I made: What was I thinking?" Mark said. "There were lots of moments my actions weren't appropriate. Expectations. He was 5, 6 and 7 playing against kids that were two years older and I expected him to perform the same way."

Understand that Mark's demands were steeped in knowledge. He coaches at the Beacon School in Manhattan, runs his own youth training ground, Global Professional Sports, and used to coach in the renowned Riverside Church program.

From his dad, and from older, unforgiving opponents

on the Amateur Athletic Union circuit and at New York's storied Dyckman Park and Rucker Park, Ty learned the game's nuances: angles, leverage, body position.

"There's someone physically trying to stop you from getting somewhere," Mark said. "And it's someone who's more athletic, stronger and faster and at a young age you have to become so crafty to make your path."

Ty refined those skills at Iona Prep in New Rochelle N.Y., where he was all-state as a junior before hip surgery short-circuited his senior year. He's grown into his frame at Virginia and is sneaky strong and athletic, but crafty and cerebral remain apt descriptions.

He's a clever passer, especially on pick-and-rolls, and leads the ACC in assists at 5.3 per game. His assist-to-turnover ratio of 3.18 ranks seventh nationally, and his ball-handling has improved considerably, thanks in part to an offseason week at Chris Paul's Elite Guard Camp — NBA scouts attend the camp, and Ty deflects questions on whether he'll explore professional options after this season.

"He's so composed," Louisville coach Chris Mack said. "His ability to read a ball screen, use those little hook passes with a couple seconds left in the shot clock, not too many college players can make that play."

Jerome's shooting range extends far beyond the NBA's 3-point line, and he's developed a mid-range game. No matter the defender's size, he has an uncanny ability to make leaners and floaters in the lane.

At 13 points per game, Jerome's scoring average is third among the Cavaliers behind De'Andre Hunter and Kyle Guy, but no one on the roster takes, or makes, more big shots than Jerome. In short, he's fearless.

His final-minute 3-pointer in last season's victory at Duke, off a wicked ball fake, will live in Virginia lore. Jerome is also partial to his clinching jumper in the 2018 ACC tournament final against North

Ty Jerome's consistency, composure and well-rounded skill set have earned him attention as an NBA prospect.

Carolina, and let's not forget the turn-around 3-pointer off the dribble — the degree of difficulty was off the charts — with 6.1 seconds remaining in last year's epic comeback at Louisville.

"My dad always preached to me, 'Never let anyone take your confidence away,'" Jerome said. "So throughout the course of a game, if I'm 0 for 12 and the game's on the line, I'm still going to want to shoot it because my confidence stays the same. I think it comes from all the work I've put in. If I'm going to put in all that work each and every single day, during the summer, during the offseason, why would I shy away from the moment when it's finally here?

"Another factor is just the confidence my team and coaches give to me. If your teammates and your coaches don't have confidence in you, you're not going to want to take that shot. … If they can have confidence in me, how can I not have confidence in myself?"

Jerome was third-team All-ACC last season and finished behind teammates Devon Hall (second team) and Guy (first team) in voting by coaches and media. He was second-team this year while Hunter and Guy made first team.

He was undervalued both times.

"He is what makes this team go," Guy said. "Obviously it's a biased opinion, but I think a lot of people would agree with me: If someone should have been on first-team All-ACC it should have been him."

"Jerome is as good a point guard or lead guard as there is in this league," Pittsburgh coach Jeff Capel said. "I think the two greatest strengths that he has are his competitiveness and his mind."

Those traits are a reflection of Mark Jerome. He still coaches Ty, breaking down video of Virginia games and offering suggestions, much like he does

with Ty's brother, Kobe, a sophomore at Bergen Catholic in North Jersey.

Those coaching sessions have become far tamer over the years.

"I don't want to make it seem like it was all bad," Mark said. "There were a lot of good times, a lot of great games. But my expectations were so high."

Ty has exceeded all expectations at U.Va., and this season the Cavaliers (31-3) have used his fire to fuel a run to the ACC regular-season title, the South Region's top seed and Thursday's semifinals.

"It means everything to me, honestly," Ty said. "It's my first time in the Sweet 16. … Everyone is talking about a Final Four, but I've never been to a Sweet 16. Just the opportunity to play with this group again for a whole 'nother week and practicing with this group and traveling with this group, that's what means the most, I think."

It's all come under Mark Jerome's watchful eye. He attended Virginia's first- and second-round tournament games last week in Columbia, S.C. — Ty averaged 12.5 points and 4.5 assists, and shot 50 percent from the field in the victories over Gardner-Webb and Oklahoma — and will be in Louisville this week, cheering alongside other proud parents.

Neither father nor son would have it any other way. This is, after all, about love.

"It's constant," Ty said of Mark's coaching, "but it's not in a demeaning way anymore. He always says he's my biggest fan and my biggest critic." ■

Ty Jerome drives past Purdue's Carsen Edwards during the second half of the NCAA tournament South Regional final game.

Virginia 69, North Carolina 61
February 11, 2019 • Chapel Hill, North Carolina

RIGHT GUY, RIGHT TIME

Junior's late heroics, U.Va.'s defensive tenacity pave way to 69-61 win at UNC

By Norm Wood

Despite all the turnovers through the first 28 minutes and all the mental lapses early in the second half North Carolina used to its advantage, Virginia coach Tony Bennett had a sense a big spark was coming from a familiar source.

Kyle Guy was ready for the moment.

Guy ignited a U.Va. rally Monday night from a seven-point deficit in the final 7½ minutes, leading the Cavaliers to a 69-61 victory at North Carolina.

He scored 11 points in the final nine minutes to help No. 4 U.Va. (21-2, 9-2 ACC) bounce back about 48 hours after losing Saturday at home against Duke. UNC was held to a season low in points.

"He's always one shot away from getting it going," Bennett said.

"He made two (3-pointers) in the last two minutes or minute-and-a-half or somewhere in there — significant. We were trying to get him to those shots, for sure, and he delivered."

De'Andre Hunter and Guy both scored 20 points to lead U.Va., which made 11 of 20 shots from 3-point range. Guy was 5 of 9 on 3s, including a pair from long range in the final two minutes that gave U.Va. the lead for good.

With the win, U.Va. is tied with UNC for second in the ACC. Duke is the only team in the league with one conference loss.

Freshman Coby White paced No. 8 UNC (19-5, 9-2) with 17 points, while Cameron Johnson added 16 points. UNC used a 17-3 second-half run to grab a 49-43 advantage, but it couldn't sustain its good fortune.

UNC connected on only 35.4 percent of its shots from the floor for the game, and missed 10 of its last 11 attempts. U.Va. made 53.3 percent of its shots.

Trailing 55-48 with 7:51 left, U.Va. went on a quick 7-0 run in less than two minutes to tie the game. Ty Jerome, who had 15 points and 11 assists and showed no ill effects from a back injury he said after the Duke game was giving him problems, made a 3-pointer with 6:09 left to tie the game at 55.

U.Va. committed 10 turnovers, marking the fourth straight game in which it gave the ball away at least 10 times, but the Cavaliers took care of it when it mattered most. They didn't commit a turnover in the final 12 minutes, 23 seconds.

After Jerome's tying 3-pointer, the teams traded baskets for the next three minutes, but White had an opportunity to provide UNC with what could've been an enormous momentum boost.

With the score tied 59-59, and as the game clock rolled under 3½ minutes, White found himself in a bind near midcourt with the shot clock displaying just one second left. He hoisted a desperate 3-pointer and

North Carolina's Kenny Williams attempts to guard Virginia's Kyle Guy during the second half. Guy scored 20 points in the 69-61 win, including some key 3-pointers late in the game.

appeared to score, but the shot was negated after an official review revealed he didn't let go of it before the shot clock expired.

Guy finally gave U.Va. some breathing room with 1:57 left via a contested 3-pointer from the deep right corner that put the Cavaliers up 64-59.

"I don't need much time to shoot," said Guy, whose shooting led the way to a 12-2 U.Va. run to finish the game. "That's something I've worked for."

As dramatic as that 3-pointer was at the time, he made another 3 soon after that deflated the Dean E. Smith Center crowd. Rising up with 1:10 remaining, Guy released a 3-pointer, made it and got fouled by Kenny Williams in the process.

Guy missed the ensuing free throw for what would've been a four-point play, but his fifth successful 3-pointer of the game gave U.Va. a 67-61 advantage. UNC went ice-cold shooting in the final minute and couldn't recover.

"We had a great run for eight to 10 minutes, or whatever it was, and things were going our way," UNC coach Roy Williams said. "After that, it got a lot more difficult. … I would like to have some of those possessions over."

Before he got hot in the closing nine minutes, Guy had misfired on five of his previous six shots from the floor. He made six of his last seven shots.

True to form, UNC dominated in the rebounding category, posting a 38-27 overall advantage and 16-3 cushion in offensive rebounds.

Though UNC outscored U.Va. 15-2 in second-chance points, the Tar Heels couldn't keep up with the Cavaliers shooting from the perimeter. UNC was 6-of-15 shooting on 3s in the opening half, which ended with U.Va. up 36-29, but the Tar Heels made only 3 of 15 from beyond the 3-point line in the second half.

"There's no excuses," Jerome said of U.Va.'s success Monday working on short rest. "I told the team before the game, 'I don't care if we played Duke on Saturday, I don't care if we're on the road (Monday). Every game we come out and we expect to win.' No matter where we are, and no matter who we're playing against." ∎

U.Va. forward Jay Huff drives to the basket, guarded by UNC's Cameron Johnson.

Virginia 73, Louisville 68
March 9, 2019 • Charlottesville, Virginia

BACK ON TOP

U.Va. rallies against Louisville, locks up top seed in ACC tournament

By Norm Wood

Two weeks ago, a bad back frustrated Ty Jerome at Louisville. No aches or pains were evident Saturday, as Jerome propelled Virginia to a 73-68 win against Louisville, clinching the top seed in the Atlantic Coast Conference tournament for the Cavaliers for the fourth time since 2014.

Jerome's 24 points, his ACC season high, helped No. 2 U.Va. (28-2, 16-2) rally from a second-half deficit.

"After I shot so badly at (Louisville), I was real excited to play them again, and they're a great defensive team and a really good team overall, too," said Jerome, who scored a season-low four points on 2-of-12 shooting from the floor Feb. 23 in U.Va.'s 64-52 win at Louisville. "My back has been getting better and better, and I'm pretty much 100 percent now."

Trailing 59-55 with just more than seven minutes left Saturday, U.Va. responded with a 13-3 run sparked by 3-pointers from Kyle Guy, Jay Huff and Braxton Key. Guy finished with 13 points.

Huff, who had nine points (on 3-of-3 shooting from beyond the 3-point line) in 12 minutes off the bench, played a huge role in the second half. U.Va. had fallen behind 55-49 before his 3-pointer with 10:18 left trimmed the deficit and ignited the crowd.

He followed his 3-pointer with blocks on back-to-back Louisville possessions. With 5:10 left, he took a pass from Jerome and knocked down another 3-pointer

from the top of the key to put the Cavaliers ahead 66-62.

Louisville (19-12, 10-8), which led by as many as seven points early in the second half, never got back within four points after U.Va. took a 68-62 lead via its big run that concluded on a jumper by Jerome with 3:36 remaining.

U.Va., which celebrated its ACC run by cutting down a net after the game while the majority of the crowd stayed and cheered, shot just 40 percent from the floor, but it made 43 percent of its 3-point attempts (12 of 28). Louisville, which got 19 points from Jordan Nwora, made 40 percent of its field-goal attempts.

Nwora was one of four double-figure scorers for Louisville, which also got 12 points from Malik Williams and 10 points each from Dwayne Sutton and Christen Cunningham.

"(U.Va. is) very impressive," said Louisville coach Chris Mack, whose team missed nine of its last 11 shots from the floor. "They're incredibly well-coached. ... We put ourselves in a position to win the game. I thought (U.Va.'s) composure versus our composure in the last three or four minutes probably decided the game."

Jerome, who was 8-of-14 shooting from the floor, made 3 of 4 shots in the second half and helped pick up the slack in a game that saw guard De'Andre Hunter struggle. He was 3-of-13 shooting from the floor and finished with just nine points, including one in the second half.

U.Va. players celebrate the school's fourth consecutive ACC regular-season title.

Playing in his final game in John Paul Jones Arena, U.Va. senior center Jack Salt started, but played just 12 minutes.

Though Salt didn't score, and spent a lot of time sitting on the bench with a heating pad against his own bad back, Jerome said after the game that winning Saturday for Salt was more important than getting the victory to nail down the top seed in the ACC tournament.

"That was a physical game," U.Va. coach Tony Bennett said. "The possessions were hard. They made some tough, contested shots. They attacked us. They made it hard for us, and that was a possession game. To be in a tough physical game, and (Hunter) wasn't scoring like he typically does — I thought Ty was terrific, obviously, and Kyle, what Jay did coming off the bench with those 3s and then Braxton making the big 3 and getting some rebounds — again, we needed all those things." ∎

25
FORWARD

MAMADI DIAKITE

Diakite made a vow to his coach: "I'm ready." He's been indispensable since.

By Norm Wood • April 2, 2019

Not long after Virginia's 69-59 loss to Florida State in the ACC tournament semifinals, Mamadi Diakite asked for a few minutes of coach Tony Bennett's time. Diakite had to clear the air.

After a conference tournament that saw him come off the bench against both North Carolina State and FSU, fail to play more than 13 minutes in either game and shoot a combined 2 of 7 for five points to go with no rebounds or blocks, Diakite had to let Bennett know he was still engaged. There would be no pouting, no sulking heading into the NCAA tournament.

"I can't exactly remember the words, but he said, 'I'm ready,' " said Bennett, who will lead his team Saturday in Minneapolis against Auburn in the Cavaliers' first Final Four appearance since 1984. "He said, 'That wasn't my best. I wasn't quite where I needed to be or right in that ACC tournament. I desperately want to do anything, absolutely anything I can to make this team advance. I know what last year was. … This is what I'm so committed to.'

"In his words, it wasn't like 'I'm back,' but it was more like 'I'm ready and I understand that I wasn't what I was in other games.' … It was an interesting conversation."

Diakite has lived up to his vow.

His last-second shot Saturday from about 12 feet away to tie U.Va.'s Sweet 16 matchup against Purdue in regulation in an eventual 80-75 overtime win left an indelible memory. But Diakite's NCAA tournament performance has been defined by more than just one shot.

He's arguably been U.Va.'s most consistent and indispensable player in the tournament. Averaging 13 points, nine rebounds and 2.3 blocks while shooting 64.9 percent from the floor (24 of 37) in four games, Diakite has been sharp on both ends of the floor.

Coming into U.Va.'s second-round game against Oklahoma, Diakite had started just once in the Cavaliers' previous 11 games, at least partially because of matchup concerns. The morning of the game against Oklahoma, and two days after he had 17 points on 8-of-10 shooting from the floor and nine rebounds in 27 minutes off the bench in a first-round win over Gardner-Webb, Diakite

Described as an X-factor early in the season, Mamadi Diakite played a critical role in Virginia's pursuit of a championship.

found out he was back in the starting lineup.

"Starting, to me, it's a big challenge," Diakite said after he posted 14 points on 7-of-9 shooting with nine rebounds and three blocks in U.Va.'s 63-51 win over Oklahoma. "(Bennett is) telling you, 'OK, you have the responsibility to help the team, and we're trusting you.' So, I just answered to it."

Diakite has remained in the starting lineup the last three games. For the most part, he's stayed out of foul trouble, which limited his minutes in the ACC tournament.

At a loss initially to describe his big shot against Purdue — he finished with 14 points, seven rebounds and four blocks — Diakite finally employed words he's used to describe teammate Ty Jerome's penchant for shooting in the clutch. Diakite, a 6-foot-9 redshirt junior from Guinea in Africa who didn't play basketball competitively until his junior year at the Blue Ridge School near Charlottesville, said his last-second shot in regulation was the product of "cold blood" — his own way of saying he had ice water in his veins.

"At the start of the season, I said Mamadi is an X-factor for us," Bennett said. "I think his talent and his ability were important, and he has improved. He's newer to the game from when he started playing. He's matured. He's had a really good season, really good outing, and I think that was the key to our success." ■

Mamadi Diakite resists pressure from Notre Dame's D.J. Harvey during a regular-season matchup. The Cavaliers defeated the Fighting Irish 82-55.

12
GUARD

DE'ANDRE HUNTER

His late father's passion, lessons helped Hunter grow into an NBA prospect

By Norm Wood • April 5, 2019

Sitting across a table from Virginia coach Tony Bennett at a Charlottesville breakfast spot early in his college career, De'Andre Hunter received a firm message about what would be required of him on both ends of the floor.

It was a one-on-one meeting, not unlike conversations Bennett has had with other players, but this chat was a bit more insistent than some. He mentioned U.Va. great Malcolm Brogdon, instantly grabbing Hunter's attention.

Bennett wanted to see the same things from Hunter he'd once asked of Brogdon, which included learning to guard players of different sizes and skill sets as Brogdon, an ACC Defensive Player of the Year, had once done. It all made sense to the 6-foot-7 Hunter, who hadn't heard an authority figure challenge him quite the same way since before his father died more than a decade earlier.

There was urgency in Bennett's tone that resonated with Hunter.

"I said, 'You know, you have something that people would die for from a basketball standpoint with your length and all that,'" said Bennett.

"I said, 'I watch Malcolm. I remember challenging Malcolm. If you can guard ones and twos and threes and fours, and really buy in and have a sense of ownership in being as great an individual defender and team defender that you can be, that'll really help this team and it'll really help you.'"

Long before he set foot in John Paul Jones Arena, Hunter established himself as a coveted recruit at Friends Central School in Wynnewood, Pa. Averaging 23.5 points, 9.8 rebounds, 2.6 assists and 2.5 blocks per game as a senior, Hunter envisioned himself capable of grasping Bennett's pack line defensive concepts right away.

It didn't work out that way. Hunter wasn't entirely prepared for the intensity of Bennett's latch-on-to-the-pack-line-or-else mentality.

"I had to learn that the hard way," said Hunter, now a redshirt sophomore who has grown into a possible top-10 pick in the NBA draft in June if he decides to leave U.Va. early.

"There's no shortcuts. If you don't defend, you're probably not going to play."

A reluctant redshirt in his first season at U.Va.,

Early in De'Andre Hunter's career, Tony Bennett challenged him to pattern his defensive game after Virginia legend Malcolm Brogdon. (Photo by Jonathon Gruenke)

Hunter learned the pack line in practice and through observation. He started to realize words of advice his father, Aaron Hunter, had repeatedly encouraged him to follow years earlier would have to become a way of life.

Aaron Hunter's message was that no matter which coach De'Andre Hunter played for, taking breaks on the court wouldn't be tolerated.

"He taught me to play hard," De'Andre Hunter said. "When I was younger, even in high school at times, I didn't play that hard sometimes. He didn't care if I scored. He didn't care about any of that. He just wanted me to play hard all the time. He taught me that at a really young age. Although I didn't really carry it through high school, I feel like in college it really molded me and really taught me a lot of things."

Arriving at U.Va. in the same recruiting class that included Kyle Guy and Ty Jerome, Hunter not only had to defensively find his niche. He also had to get comfortable with the unique collection of talent Bennett had assembled in Charlottesville — specifically, he had to get on the same page with Jerome.

"He wasn't really my favorite person," De'Andre Hunter said. "I got to know him. He's from New York, I'm from Philly, so we share a lot of common interests. He's my brother now. I'd go to war with him. I love the dude."

Chemistry is indeed no longer an issue for Hunter and Jerome. They live together and have taken all but one class together.

"We're best friends, literally brothers," Jerome said. "We still have days where we'll piss each other off all the time. That's what family does, but at the end of the day, I'll do anything for him, and I know when it comes down to it, he'll do anything for me."

Dad's passionate encouragement has always carried a lot of weight for Hunter, who eventually mastered the pack line, earning defensive player of the year honors this season from the National Association of Basketball Coaches and the ACC. His dad's inspiration still leaves an impression 14 years after his death — a topic De'Andre Hunter and his brother, also named Aaron Hunter, prefer to keep private.

"He was young," Aaron Hunter said of his brother. "I still don't even know if he quite understands it."

Aaron Hunter has heard all the stories about his dad's basketball skills in the inner-city of Philadelphia at famed Simon Gratz High — a school that produced four-time NBA All-Star Rasheed Wallace among other pro players.

"If you come to Philadelphia and go back to his old neighborhood, they still talk about him as if he played last night," said Aaron Hunter, who is 11 years older than De'Andre. "He was definitely a good player.

"I played, and I was pretty good, but my brother got that love for the game from our dad."

Dad's skills have certainly rubbed off on Hunter, a third-team Associated Press All-American this season who is averaging 14.9 points and five rebounds per game.

With a fine-tuned high post game, he's emerged as a player capable of flashing into the middle of a zone defense to knock down short jumpers, beguile defenders with a quick jab step, get to the free-throw line on drives to the basket or step back and knock down a 3-pointer.

"De'Andre Hunter is one of those multi-dimensional players, like a Kawhi Leonard, that first of all you have to give him a lot of credit for his defense," Miami coach Jim Larranaga said. "Second of all, he starts at (small forward) and can play on the perimeter, make a three, can put it on the ground and take a guy one-on-one. ... He can post up. He can turn and face from the post and jab at you, jab at you and make a little 12 to 15 footer."

Larranaga isn't the first to compare Hunter to Leonard, and while the assumption is a jump to the NBA awaits Hunter after this season, he's been tight-lipped

Hunter averaged 14.9 points and five rebounds per game on his way to a third-team Associated Press All-American selection.

about his future.

What if the draft gurus have him pegged as a sure-fire lottery pick at the end of spring?

"I don't know," Hunter said. "I'll have to see when it's June and see if they're saying that."

Regardless of Hunter's choice after the season, his brother has made sure to remind him his earliest mentor in the game would be overjoyed by his success.

"To be honest, he hasn't said one word about it," Aaron Hunter said about his brother's decision to turn pro. "Not one. I even sat down and sent him a message about it, and he didn't respond.

"I have made sure to tell him, 'Yo, man. If I've never told you, I want to let you know our father would be so proud of you, and he'd be jumping for joy to see where his son is at.' I said, 'I know he can't tell you, but I'll most definitely tell you that I'm proud of you.' "

Hearing it from his big brother means a lot, but nothing replaces a father's love.

"There's days I just wish he could be here and watch me play in college," Hunter said. "I know that was a dream of his to see me to do that. I know he'd be so proud."

Just before the start of the ACC tournament in early March, Bennett met again with Hunter.

This time, Bennett's point was far more basic, but just as heartfelt.

"I told him how thankful I was and proud of him I was that he's embracing that," Bennett said. "Not perfect, but we talked about that. I let him know, I said, 'Look, you were the Defensive Player of the Year in the ACC and you made first team (All-ACC). Remember we sat in this restaurant two years, I can't remember exactly how long ago, so I like that. ... You've got to be able to play both sides of the ball. You just have to. That's the way the game has gone nowadays.' " ■

Hunter's all-around game allowed him to contribute in notable fashion even when shots weren't falling for him at times in the NCAA Tournament.

ACC Tournament Quarterfinal

Virginia 76, North Carolina State 56
March 14, 2019 • Charlotte, North Carolina

ALL IN GOOD TIME

U. Va. overcomes slow start, blows out N.C. State

By Norm Wood

Early in the ACC tournament quarterfinal against North Carolina State, Virginia center Jack Salt failed to corral an offensive rebound that was within his reach. Cavaliers guard Ty Jerome felt it was time for a heart-to-heart.

He let Salt have it.

"I turned to him and said, 'You know you've got to box out, right?'" Jerome said. "He gave me this look like, 'Come on. That's what I do.' "

Maybe it was the pep talk, maybe it was self-motivation or maybe it was just Salt's time in top seed U.Va.'s 76-56 win against No. 8 seed N.C. State. Whatever it was, he put a slow start behind him and balanced U.Va. guard Kyle Guy's perimeter-driven 29 points with an interior game that produced a career-high 18 points.

U.Va. (29-2) advanced to play in the semifinals against No. 4 seed Florida State. It's the fifth time in the last six seasons the Cavaliers have made it to at least the semifinals.

U.Va., which won 66-65 in overtime at N.C. State in January, rallied from a 29-27 halftime deficit Thursday behind big second-half efforts from Guy, Salt and De'Andre Hunter, who had 16 points for the game. The trio combined to score 43 of U.Va.'s 49 points in the second half, offsetting Jerome's off shooting day (two points on 1-of-11 from the floor to go along with 10 assists and four steals).

Cavaliers coach Tony Bennett joked he might honor New Zealand native Salt's heritage after the game with a traditional Kiwi dance.

"I thought (Guy and Salt) were terrific (Wednesday)," said Bennett, whose team made 52.1 percent of its field-goal attempts. "I even joked with the guys, I think I'm going to do a haka in the locker room the way Jack played."

Guy connected on 7 of 9 shots from 3-point range on his way to finishing one-point shy of tying his career scoring high. Despite his shooting performance, he deflected attention to the Cavaliers' 6-foot-10 senior center.

"You guys need to be interviewing him, not me," Guy said to reporters after the game in U.Va.'s locker room. "He's the player of the game. He did all the little things, and I think after about four minutes in the first half, he was frustrated with himself. He missed (a layup) and wasn't boxing out or playing as hard as he could, so he really proved us all right with what we know he could do in the second half."

Before the quarterfinal, Salt had scored in double figures just three times in his career, with his career high of 12 points coming Nov. 28 in U.Va.'s win at Maryland. A trio of three-point plays, which accounted for the majority of the career 45.7 percent free-throw shooter's 4-of-5 effort Thursday from the line, highlighted Salt's huge afternoon.

Kyle Guy maneuvers under the basket against N.C. State. Guy led Virginia with 29 points.

With U.Va. trailing 31-27, and 18 minutes left, Salt grabbed an offensive rebound off a missed 3-pointer by Guy. Starting from near the 3-point line on the left side of the court, Salt surprisingly put the ball on the floor with his left hand, drove past N.C. State's Wyatt Walker, scored on a reverse layup, got fouled by Walker and made the ensuing free throw.

"I think (Walker) was kind of expecting me to pass it, which is what I usually do when I get an offensive rebound," said Salt, who showed no ill effects from a recurring back injury that has bothered him this season, making 7 of 8 shots from the floor for the game and scoring 15 points in the second half.

"There's a lot of really strong guys in this conference, but he's up there. ...To be able to make that move on him was good."

After a dunk with 7:38 left that put U.Va. ahead 59-43, Salt hung on the rim and was called for a technical foul by official Jamie Luckie — an acceptable foible for Salt given his overall effort.

N.C. State (22-11), which shot 38.8 percent from the floor and was led by Markell Johnson's 13 points, fell behind 16-6 with 13:20 left in the first half before it went on an 18-2 run over the course of five minutes to build a six-point lead — its largest of the game.

A 22-5 run in the second half fueled by 12 points from Guy, including a four-point play (3-pointer and successful free throw), helped U.Va. take a 57-41 lead with just more than eight minutes left. Its lead never fell under 14 points the rest of the way.

"You look at that stat line, but he's deceptive with that as far as getting in there (to the basket)," Bennett said regarding Guy. "I thought he made some terrific passes to guys, and he's unselfish, so yes, that's a triple threat." ∎

Jack Salt slams one down during the first half. The senior center scored 18 as Virginia advanced to the ACC tournament semifinal.

ACC Tournament Semifinal

Florida State 69, Virginia 59
March 15, 2019 • Charlotte, North Carolina

ROLE REVERSAL

FSU "tougher" than U.Va. in semifinal

By David Teel

Virginia played far from its best in Friday's ACC tournament loss to Florida State. But make no mistake, the overlooked Seminoles were exceptional.

Long and quick, Florida State excelled at both ends, affecting U.Va. shots near and far. Moreover, the Seminoles carved up the Cavaliers' defense like few others, shooting 56.5 percent in the 69-59 semifinal victory.

Only Duke (57.8 percent) has been more accurate against Virginia (29-3) this season.

Shocked? You shouldn't be. Florida State (27-6) has won 14 of its last 15 games with a roster that includes the core of last year's Elite Eight squad.

In short, this was one quality team besting another.

"I don't think there any upsets in the ACC anymore," Seminoles coach Leonard Hamilton said.

Not quite, but to be sure, this was of the mild variety, simply because the Cavaliers, still destined for a No. 1 seed in next week's NCAA tournament, have been so consistent.

But Virginia seemed a half-step slow Friday, or maybe Florida State was a half-step quicker than usual. The Seminoles smothered Cavaliers guards Ty Jerome and Kyle Guy, limiting them to 7-of-21 shooting, 4 of 14 beyond the 3-point arc.

Guy, who scored 29 points in Thursday's quarterfinal win over North Carolina State, had 11 Friday, none in a second half when he attempted only two shots. Jerome scored 10 points, eight more than Thursday, but shot 5 of 25 for the tournament. Getting him right for the NCAAs is the Cavaliers' primary task in the next week.

Virginia defeated FSU 65-52 in the ACC opener for both Jan. 5, but the game was a blowout. The Cavaliers led by 29 before the Seminoles closed the gap against U.Va.'s walk-ons. No Florida State player scored in double figures, and the Seminoles had as turnovers (15) as field goals.

Friday was a reversal. Reserve guard David Nichols, a 38.5-percent shooter on the season, went 6 for 8 and led four FSU double-figure scorers with 14 points.

Illustrating the Seminoles' depth: Terance Mann and Devin Vassell, who hit the essential shots in their quarterfinal victory over Virginia Tech, combined for only two points Friday.

But that's how FSU rolls. No Seminole averages more than 13 points a game, and none made any of the three All-ACC teams — Mfiondu Kabengele was the Sixth Man of the Year — but nine played at least 11 minutes Friday.

Florida State's Trent Forrest drives past Kihei Clark during the second half. Forrest contributed 10 points, one of four Seminoles to score in double figures as FSU advanced to the conference championship game.

"Part of it was they were so good offensively," Virginia forward Jay Huff said of the Cavaliers' defensive issues. "The loss makes it feel a lot worse."

Virginia missed its first eight 3-point attempts and trailed by as many as 10 in the first half before Guy hit two from beyond the arc to help the Cavaliers draw within 35-31 at intermission.

The Cavaliers led briefly during the second half and were down 49-48 after Jerome's 3-pointer off a nasty dribble shake of M.J. Walker. But the Seminoles countered with a 13-1 binge to regain command. Nichols scored eight of those 13 points.

"We had a lot of breakdowns and things that if you want to win just can't happen," said All-ACC forward De'Andre Hunter, Virginia's leading scorer Friday with 13 points.

"They were just the tougher team tonight," Jerome said. "More physical tonight. All of it."

This is the 66th ACC tournament but the first semifinals to showcase three top-five Associated Press teams: No. 2 Virginia, No. 3 North Carolina and No. 5 Duke. Oh, and Florida State is No. 12.

"Anytime this league in basketball has something happen that's never been done before, it's pretty remarkable," ACC commissioner John Swofford said prior to tipoff.

The Seminoles face the Duke-Carolina winner in Saturday's 8:30 p.m. championship game.

Meanwhile, Virginia will be back in Charlottesville, preparing for Sunday's NCAA bracket reveal and a return to the event that broke the program's heart last year with a first-round loss to UMBC.

"We're focused enough and we've been around the block a few times," Huff said. "I think we'll be just fine."

To close on a light note: A reporter asked Virginia coach Tony Bennett during the postgame news conference whether he subscribes to the notion that a setback at this stage could help a team in the NCAA tournament.

"I do now," he said. ∎

Virginia's Mamadi Diakite drives to the basket during the first half.

LEARNING FROM DEFEAT

U. Va. owns loss and grows as a result

By David Teel • March 21, 2019

As ESPN's Twitter account duly noted, March 16 was the one-year anniversary of Virginia's historic NCAA tournament demise against UMBC. Kyle Guy was among those who retweeted the memory.

When Duke students started a GoFundMe account to fly former UMBC guard K.J. Maura to January's U.Va.-Duke game at Cameron Indoor Stadium with the express aim to "make Kyle Guy weep," Guy on Twitter implored Cavaliers fans to "make this happen."

That is the genius of Virginia's program: Players and coaches have owned their failure, learned from it and authored yet another indelible regular season.

And here they are again, a No. 1 NCAA regional seed preparing to face another No. 16, this time Big South tournament champion Gardner-Webb. Do not expect anything resembling a sequel.

The Cavaliers are too good, too focused, too at peace with March 16, 2018, when they became the first No. 1 to lose to a No. 16 — by 20 points, no less.

"I don't think anyone's ever going to forget about it, including me," said Guy, U.Va.'s first-team All-ACC guard.

Taking their cue from head coach Tony Bennett, Guy and backcourt mate Ty Jerome have led Virginia's coping with UMBC, on and off the court. And fate conspired with opposing fans — Maura did not make it to Cameron — to help them with constant reminders.

Where was the ACC's preseason media day? At the same Charlotte, N.C., arena where the Cavaliers fell to the Retrievers.

Bennett, Guy and senior center Jack Salt attended the event and were assigned the same hotel they stayed in prior to UMBC. They were greeted like old friends by the hotel staff.

And where was last week's ACC tournament? Back in Charlotte, where once again media asked about UMBC.

March 16 was the ACC title game, and Guy contemplated what an irresistible story it would be if Virginia cut down the nets one year to the day after UMBC. Instead, the Cavaliers fell to Florida State in the semifinals, and Duke won the title a night later.

But a conference championship would not have quieted the UMBC chatter, just as U.Va.'s regular-season ACC title did not. Since the final horn last March in Charlotte, this season has been about NCAA tournament redemption.

"I would be lying if I told you I wasn't looking forward to this all year," Jerome said, "because in the back of my mind, it was about getting back to this position and avenging last year."

Jerome needed about 10 days of decompression last March before watching tape of the UMBC game, and his primary takeaway was painfully succinct.

"I had to get so much better," he said, "and we had to get so much better. That was the biggest thing. We've done a pretty good job of that so far."

No doubt. The Cavaliers (29-3) lost only to Duke (twice) and FSU. They set a conference record with five road victories over top-25 opponents and earned a No. 1 NCAA seed for the fourth time in six years.

"And now," Jerome said, "it's time to keep improving."

Starting Friday. Competing in the Division I NCAA tournament for the first time, Gardner-Webb (23-11) tied for third in the Big South and has effective 3-point shooters at every position. Moreover, the Bulldogs defeated lower-tier ACC teams Georgia Tech

Kyle Guy helps cut down the net after Virginia's overtime win over Purdue to advance to the Final Four.

and Wake Forest.

"No disrespect to those programs," Gardner-Webb coach Tim Craft said, "but Virginia is a different animal for sure."

A wounded one at that, wounded but clearly not deterred by UMBC.

Retrievers coach Ryan Odom was so impressed by Virginia's and Guy's ownership of the result that he wrote Guy a letter saying he is rooting for U.Va. Echoing Odom, Bennett and Craft applauded the Cavaliers' handling of their unique setback.

During podium interviews Thursday, 12 of 27 questions to Bennett and his players were about UMBC. Nine of the 28 to Craft and the Bulldogs were about UMBC.

"I feel like they'll come out with a vengeance," Gardner-Webb guard David Efianayi said.

Thousands of miles away in Salt Lake City, where West Region No. 1 Gonzaga is competing, UMBC was mentioned, and Friday's television crew of Jim Nantz, Grant Hill, Bill Raftery and Tracy Wolfson, the same foursome that worked the Cavaliers-Retrievers game, is sure to reference it early and often.

"I would say in practice, whenever somebody's tired, or you're trying to fight through a rep or take a play off or something, I always think back to that," Guy said. "And then when I'm on the court, I don't even think about it. I'm focused on what's in front of me because, if you're too focused on the past, you're not going to be able to move forward.

"So, yeah, it's a chip on our shoulder, but it doesn't define us. We're just trying to move past it and let the inspiration and motivation behind it take us somewhere we haven't been. ... We're ready to put on a show this year so we can talk about something else."

The journey starts Friday in Columbia, and the Cavaliers aspire to end it at the Final Four in Minneapolis.

"We're in charge of our story now," Guy said. ∎

Virginia players (from left) Ty Jerome, Kyle Guy, De'Andre Hunter and Mamadi Diakite celebrate on the bench during the second half of the Cavaliers' 81-51 home win over Georgia Tech.

NCAA Tournament First Round

Virginia 71, Gardner-Webb 56
March 22, 2019 • Columbia, South Carolina

BURDEN LIFTED

U.Va. finds its "edge" in second half to defeat Gardner-Webb

By David Teel

College basketball history is littered with Final Four teams that struggled in the NCAA tournament's first round. Virginia hopes to join that group — Duke 1986, Syracuse '87 and Kentucky 2011 are among the others — after Friday's 71-56 victory over Gardner-Webb.

Sure, the Cavaliers led by double-digit margins for the final 11-plus minutes and by as many as 21 points. But as any witness will attest, Virginia in no way resembled a No. 1 regional seed and ACC regular-season champion in the first half.

What the Cavaliers instead resembled was the defenseless bunch that last season became the first No. 1 seed to lose to a No. 16 in the first round, by 20 points to UMBC.

With that burden, what must U.Va.'s players, coaches and fans have been thinking when Gardner-Webb led 30-16? How badly must their insides have been churning?

Did Virginia need adjustments or a collective dose of Pepto? That's a pressure only the Cavaliers can understand.

"I can't speak for everyone," guard Ty Jerome said, "but for me I think it creeped in once, it creeped in twice, and then I just tuned it out and used it as fuel."

How could it not? But the Cavaliers (30-3) are accustomed to comebacks on the road. They rallied from seven down in the final eight-plus minutes at North Carolina. They erased a 12-point, first-half deficit and prevailed at Louisville.

And make no mistake, Friday's game at the University of South Carolina was a virtual road game for U.Va. Gardner-Webb's Boiling Springs, N.C., campus is about a two-hour drive from Columbia, and the entire town seemed shoehorned into the arena for the Bulldogs' first NCAA Division I tournament appearance.

Moreover, as Gardner-Webb (23-12), the Big South tournament champs and the league's third-place team in the regular season, built its advantage, impartial spectators climbed aboard the bandwagon. The Cavaliers only egged them on.

Careless on offense, Virginia committed five consecutive turnovers during one unsightly first-half stretch. Most uncharacteristic: They defended poorly inside and out.

But Virginia drew within 36-30 at halftime on Kihei Clark's 3-pointer, which Cavaliers coach Tony Bennett called "pivotal."

"Halftime was super-calm," Jerome said. "It was all about adjustments. … There was no rah-rah, no 'don't let this happen again.' … We made it about basketball."

Bennett: "Yes, we made some adjustments that I think helped the guys out there, but it was, 'don't you dare leave anything in this locker room.'"

The Cavaliers didn't, opening the second half on a 25-5 binge.

Ty Jerome shoots over Gardner-Webb's Jose Perez during the first-round Virginia win. Jerome had 13 points and six assists in the victory.

Clark, reserve Braxton Key and ACC Defensive Player of the Year De'Andre Hunter ignited a defense that began switching ball screens and clogging passing lanes. Hunter scored a game-high 23 points, 17 after halftime, and Mamadi Diakite added 17 points, one shy of his career-high.

A projected NBA lottery pick, Hunter missed the UMBC setback with a broken wrist. His presence Friday, his ability to create offense virtually at will and to defend multiple positions, was invaluable.

"He's the only guy on the team that has an (isolation) play called for him," Jerome said of Hunter.

Gardner-Webb has no such talent, and the Bulldogs committed 12 of their 16 turnovers after intermission. Guard Jose Perez scored 19 points on the afternoon, but forward DJ Laster missed all five of his second-half shots and went scoreless after 10 first-half points.

Virginia advances to a second-round game Sunday against ninth-seeded Oklahoma. The Sooners dismantled Ole Miss from start to finish Friday, winning 95-68.

The Cavaliers approached similar efficiency Friday only after falling behind by two touchdowns.

"We had an author come and talk to us last year, Joshua Medcalf," guard Kyle Guy said, "and one of the things he said always stuck with me, is be where your feet are. So some of those outside pressures that can creep into our minds (are) all external, and it comes from thinking too much about the future, too much about the past. So we just tried to be where our feet were."

Jerome recalled the panic of halftime against UMBC, though that game was 21-all at intermission.

"That was one thing I remember," he said, "not doing a good job keeping everyone calm. That's what I pride myself on, too. Every timeout, it's just a matter of keeping guys calm, keeping guys calm, but also keeping our edge. You've got to find a balance. You can't come out (and say), 'Everything's going to be OK. Stay calm.' Just trying to find the right balance of staying calm and keeping our edge."

The Cavaliers will need their edge for the entire 40 minutes Sunday and beyond. No more first-half mulligans. ■

De'Andre Hunter drives to the hoop against Gardner-Webb. Hunter had a huge game, scoring 23 points and pulling down six rebounds.

NCAA Tournament Second Round

Virginia 63, Oklahoma 51
March 24, 2019 • Columbia, South Carolina

LATER, SOONERS!

Diakite excels as U. Va. tops Oklahoma, advances to Sweet 16

By David Teel

Mamadi Diakite played his best game in a Virginia uniform Friday in the NCAA tournament against Gardner-Webb. Sunday he was better.

His numbers weren't better, but he was, and that's largely why the Cavaliers are headed back to the Sweet 16.

Virginia defeated Oklahoma 63-51 on a night when its two first-team All-ACC players, De'Andre Hunter and Kyle Guy, shot poorly. Diakite did not. Moreover, the 6-foot-9 redshirt junior defended and rebounded fiercely.

His final numbers: 14 points on 7-of-9 shooting, nine rebounds and three blocked shots.

Still a hoops fledgling after spending much of his youth in his native Guinea, Diakite has unlimited potential, and man did he show it this weekend.

Coming off the bench Friday in the first round against Gardner-Webb, he scored 17 points, one shy of his career-high, and matched his career-best with nine rebounds, earning his first start in seven games — he replaced Jack Salt.

Diakite's two-game tournament aggregate in Columbia: 31 points on 15-of-18 shooting, 18 rebounds and three blocks.

"I've just been very patient and letting the game come to me," he said.

"When Mamadi's locked in, he's as talented as they come," Virginia guard Ty Jerome said. "He finishes through contact and above people. He's calm. He's confident with the ball. … He was special defending against (Kristian) Doolittle."

Doolittle finished with 10 points and five rebounds, far shy of the 19 and 15 he produced in the Sooners' 95-72 first-round victory over Ole Miss.

Oklahoma (20-14) shot 57.6 percent against the Rebels, 36.5 against the Cavaliers.

Top-seeded in the South Region, Virginia (31-3) has matched the school record for victories established last season and prepares for Thursday's South Regional semifinals in Louisville, Ky., against 12th-seeded Oregon.

Virginia led 31-22 after a first half that was quintessential Cavaliers' defense and the polar opposite of Oklahoma's rout of Ole Miss. With six points, five rebounds and three blocked shots in two minutes, Diakite was the best and most active player on the court, his athleticism and energy evident with most every step.

The Sooners' final chance to create serious tension in the second half vanished with about 8:15 remaining. And Diakite again was central.

With Virginia leading 48-37, Diakite forced Doolittle into an errant shot, which Diakite rebounded. Seconds

Mamadi Diakite attacks the basket and scores while defended by Oklahoma's Matt Freeman during Virginia's 63-51 win. Diakite powered the team with 14 points and nine rebounds.

later, Diakite dunked off a perfect lob from Braxton Key.

A source of concern for the Cavaliers moving forward: Guy missed all 10 of his 3-point attempts Sunday and 14 of his 15 for the two games. He'll need to heat up if Virginia is to reach its first Final Four since 1984.

Following an Elite Eight appearance in 1995 under Jeff Jones, Virginia did not reach the NCAA tournament's second weekend for 18 consecutive years. Now Tony Bennett's program has survived the opening two rounds for the third time in six seasons.

Courtesy of conference expansion and exceptional programs, the ACC has at least five teams among the Sweet 16 for the third time in the last five seasons. A record six from the league reached the regional semifinals in 2016, five each in 2015 and this year.

Virginia Tech, Duke, North Carolina and Florida State join Virginia this season. This marks the first time since 2011, when VCU and Richmond advanced, that two state teams have made the Sweet 16.

Such postseason success often hinges on balance and unexpected contributions from those who play outside the social media microscope. That was Virginia on Sunday, and not just with Diakite.

Key, Kihei Clark and Jay Huff combined for 23 points and made nine of their 12 shots from the floor.

"An uncharacteristically cold shooting night for Kyle," Bennett said, "but they withstood that."

No one more than Diakite.

"I was trying to respond to the challenge Coach gave me," Diakite said. "He started me tonight, and I wanted to prove to him that I was ready to play."

That he was, and then some.

"We thought maybe he could play one-on-one against Doolittle," Bennett said of starting Diakite. "But what we wanted to do offensively, I thought there was some more scoring opportunities for how we were going to attack for Mamadi, how to roll and get on the rim

Big man Jay Huff stretches out for a loose ball against Oklahoma's Christian James. Huff was strong off the bench in nine minutes, chipping in five points and three rebounds.

and make some plays. And then his quickness, I thought might be a factor."

Diakite redshirted during Virginia's most recent deep tournament, to the 2016 Elite Eight. He's been eager since to contribute to a similarly memorable postseason.

Twice last year and twice during this regular season Diakite scored in double figures in back-to-back games. But never has he affected games as he did this weekend.

And never was his contribution more essential.

"I've been talking too much," Diakite said. "It's time to go, time to prove it with actions." ∎

Above: Braxton Key (2) blocks a shot attempt by Oklahoma's Aaron Calixte while Virginia's De'Andre Hunter (12) watches during the second half of the second-round win. Opposite: Ty Jerome dribbles while defended by Calixte. Jerome had 12 points, three assists and three steals in the win.

Virginia 53, Oregon 49
March 28, 2019 • Louisville, Kentucky

TY BREAKER!

Jerome's late 3, Clark's effort help Virginia get back to Elite 8

By Norm Wood

His heart pounding, legs burning, lungs screaming after more than 35 minutes of dealing with Oregon's match-up zone and switching man-to-man, Ty Jerome knew it was his time in the late stages of Virginia's Sweet 16 grind against the Ducks.

Just like last season against Duke and Louisville in the regular season or North Carolina in the ACC championship game, or even this season against VCU, Jerome's flair for the dramatic when the clock turned toward the waning minutes Thursday night helped vault South Region No. 1 seed U.Va. to a 53-49 win against No. 12 seed Oregon.

Jerome's 3-pointer with 3:34 left put U.Va. (32-3) ahead 48-45 — a lead it would make stand for the rest of the game. Before that shot, he'd only attempted three field goals in the second half and missed two of them, but none of that mattered to Jerome when he rose up for his huge 3-point shot.

"It's not like I was hot or anything at that time, but (teammates and coaches) have all the confidence in the world in me in late-game situations," Jerome said. "I can feel that. When the game's getting close, the game's getting late, I can feel guys start to look at me and give me that confidence, and that gives me all the confidence in the world."

The last time U.Va. was in the Elite Eight in 2016, it was a No. 1 seed, but couldn't get the job done. It blew a 16-point second-half lead in Chicago against No. 10 seed Syracuse, losing 68-62.

As clutch as Jerome was when U.Va. needed him most, freshman guard Kihei Clark was just as critical to the Cavaliers' success in the second half. Jerome led U.Va. with 13 points, while Clark added 12 points, reaching double figures for the first time in 16 games and the second time in his college career.

Both Jerome and Clark, who made 1 of 2 free throws with under two seconds left to give U.Va. its final four-point cushion, had six assists each. Forward Mamadi Diakite, who had seven points, a game-high 11 rebounds, two blocks and two steals, was the catalyst for U.Va.'s 34-31 edge on the boards.

Taking advantage of a late scoring drought by Oregon (25-13), which saw its 10-game winning streak snapped, U.Va. fended off the Ducks in the closing minutes.

While U.Va. didn't play one of the most aesthetically pleasing games of the tournament, it was as effective defensively as it's been all season. Oregon (25-13) shot just 37.8 percent from the floor, which was still slightly better than U.Va. (35.7 percent).

"They're tough defensively to figure out," said U.Va. coach Tony Bennett, whose team held a 7-0 first-half

Ty Jerome goes to the basket against Oregon's Louis King during Virginia's closely contested Sweet 16 win. Jerome had 13 points, six rebounds and six assists, and hit a clutch 3-pointer late to help seal the win.

advantage in offensive rebounding against Oregon's foursome of 6-foot-9 starters, using it to help build a 30-22 halftime edge. "We don't play against that a lot. At times we struggled, but made enough offensive plays, but certainly rallied defensively in the right plays."

Oregon, which held an opponent to 40 percent shooting or worse for the 10th time in its last 11 games, missed its last five shots from the floor and six of its last seven. It failed to score a field goal in the final 5 minutes, 43 seconds, including misfiring on a trio of 3-pointers in the span of 2½ minutes after it fell behind 48-45.

U.Va.'s Kyle Guy struggled again, making just 4 of 15 field-goal attempts and 2 of 11 shots from 3-point range (2 for his last 23 from 3-point range) to finish with 10 points, but Clark helped pick up the slack. His 3-pointer with 5:21 left tied the game 45-45.

Despite making only 4 of 13 shots from the floor and scoring 11 points, U.Va.'s De'Andre Hunter made

Opposite: Ty Jerome is defended by Oregon's Payton Pritchard. U.Va.'s stout defense frustrated Pritchard, who scored 11 points but needed 12 shots to do so. Above: With their win over Oregon, Tony Bennett and Virginia clinched their second Elite Eight appearance in the last four years.

it a two-possession game with 13 seconds left when he knocked down a pair of free throws.

Louis King, who paced Oregon with 16 points and made three of his four 3-pointers for the game in the second half, couldn't connect on a 3-point attempt with five seconds left. He made a pair of free throws with less than two seconds left to trim U.Va.'s lead to 52-49 — making Clark's final free throw essential.

"We're in March, and it's 40-minute territory, as Coach always tells us," Guy said. "So it helps that we try to stay calm under pressure and that we try to execute and get stops defensively, no matter what the score is or how hectic the game is going. That will always be in our advantage, and we're going to try to continue to bring that to every game." ■

Above: De'Andre Hunter was relatively quiet in the win, scoring 11 points and pulling down four rebounds. Opposite: Ty Jerome was only 5-of-12 from the floor but hit the big shot late to preserve the win for U.Va.

5

GUARD

KYLE GUY

Kyle Guy stepped to the line with three crucial free throws: "I think all of my life has led to this."

By David Teel • April 7, 2019

Hooping in the backyard with his friends, a young Kyle Guy never envisioned pressure free throws. Contested jumpers and up-and-unders? For the win? Absolutely. But not solitary free throws.

Yet if there is anyone Virginia wants at the line with championship stakes, it's the junior guard from Indianapolis — and not just because he's an 80.1 percent career foul shooter.

You know the sequence. Having butchered a late, 10-point lead in Saturday's Final Four semifinals, U.Va. trailed Auburn 62-60 when Tigers guard Samir Doughty fouled Guy as he attempted a 3-pointer with six-tenths of a second remaining.

"He is wired for what happened last night," Virginia assistant coach Brad Soderberg said Sunday. "In a game that's insignificant, if there is such a thing, he'll make six out of 10. And you're like, 'Why are you doing that? You can make them all.' But when it's the biggest — at Carolina, at Duke — bucket. Some guys are that way. He loves that."

Players, coaches, spectators, television viewers, radio listeners: Everyone was drawn to the moment.

Guy: "I think all of my life has led to this. Everything that I've been through made it a lot easier to hone in and try to knock down the free throws. I said that I was terrified. It was a good terrified, though, a good nervousness in my stomach like, 'This is my chance,' type thing. I don't know where it comes from. I know that my family's always been behind me, and I got to look at them before I shot the free throws."

Associate head coach Jason Williford: "That's big-time pressure. We left him alone. In the huddle, nobody talked to him. … He was locked in."

Junior guard Ty Jerome: "The big shots I've taken and hit in my career have been 3s mostly. They've just been quick decisions and rhythm shooting where you don't have time to think. For Kyle to go down there and calmly make three throws, after they iced him after the second one, is unreal. It's a testament to his mental toughness, confidence and focus."

Indeed, following a delay for officials to confirm how much time remained, Guy made the first two, the first as Auburn guard Bryce Brown gave the choke sign behind him. After the second, Tigers coach Bruce Pearl called timeout. More time to think.

Kyle Guy looks to the basket before attempting a 3-pointer and being fouled by Auburn's Samir Doughty at the end of the national semifinal. Guy went on to make all three of his free throws and clinched the dramatic win. (Photo by Jonathon Gruenke)

Like the first two, Guy's third free throw was pure, sending Virginia into Monday's national championship game against Texas Tech.

The only comparable Final Four moment I recall is Michigan's Rumeal Robinson going 2 for 2 from the line with three seconds left in the Wolverines' 80-79 overtime victory over Seton Hall in the 1989 title contest. Robinson was only a 64.2-percent free-throw shooter, and like Guy, had endured recent basketball hardship.

Earlier that season, with Michigan down one at Wisconsin, Robinson had missed two foul shots with seven seconds remaining. The Wolverines lost by three.

That pales to what Guy and Virginia experienced after last season's first-round NCAA tournament loss to UMBC, the first by a No. 1 seed to a No. 16. In an effort to help anyone plagued by anxiety and/or depression, Guy has courageously shared, via the written and spoken word, the mental struggles he faced post-UMBC.

So of all the young men to face that pressure Saturday night, with 72,711 in U.S. Bank Stadium howling and millions at home hyperventilating …

"After last year, I had to take a lot of time to myself," Guy said. "That's when I wrote the letters, just tried to do anything that was therapeutic for me so I could bounce back from it and be stronger as a person. I think you see the growth from that, not only with myself but with the team."

Absolutely. Down 14 in the first half two weeks ago to another 16 seed, Gardner-Webb, the Cavaliers didn't blink. Nor did they down three with 5.9 seconds remaining in regulation against Purdue in the South Regional final, or down four with 10 seconds left against Auburn.

I asked Williford, Soderberg and Virginia head coach Tony Bennett on Sunday about their most pressurized foul shots as players.

"High school I had to make two free throws to win a regional final game against George Wythe," Williford said. "In high school, that was easy. I knocked 'em down. In college, it was a different ballgame."

Kyle Guy is best known for his shooting stroke but has turned into a strong defender as well, a must for any Virginia star or rotational player alike. (Photo by Jonathon Gruenke)

Soderberg: "I made 1 for 2 at Wisconsin-Whitewater senior year. I was mad. I was an 84-percent free-throw shooter (for Wisconsin-Stevens Point). The game was on the line, inside of a minute. We ended up winning because we had a pro on our team named Terry Porter. He bailed us out. I remember that plain as day."

Bennett: "There's been a bunch of them, but I've got kind of a funny story. I got fouled, and we were maybe down two. This was at Green Bay when I played there. We were down one or down two. I went to the line, and for some reason, before I went to the line, I just looked back over my shoulder because I knew where my mom sat.

"And when I looked at my mom … she had her hands in her face. I was like, 'Oh, great.' And I remember making them, and I gave her the business ever since from that, like, 'Thanks, Mom. You're supposed to believe in your son.'"

Indiana is renowned for producing shooters, and Guy, the state's Mr. Basketball in 2016, speaks often about how all-encompassing the game is to Hoosiers. He began like many of us, hoisting two-handed set shots, until his sixth-grade guidance counselor, former Purdue football player Lee Larkins, taught him otherwise.

A two-time, first-team All-ACC selection, Guy has developed into one of the nation's best jump shooters, and his five 3-pointers after halftime against Purdue, not to mention his right-corner trey with seven seconds left versus Auburn, were XXL.

"These last two games have given me adrenaline to last a lifetime," Guy said, "and probably knocked a couple years off my life."

And he wouldn't trade them for the world.

Soderberg recalled the first time he evaluated Guy as a prospective Virginia player. He was out early for warm-ups, clowning around with his teammates.

"You watch him now," Soderberg said, "and sometimes it seems a little frivolous what he's doing in warm-ups. (But) he's having fun, and isn't that we're all supposed to do?" ■

Heavily recruited as a high school All-American, Kyle Guy has received All-American honors at the college level as well.

NCAA Tournament Elite Eight

Virginia 80, Purdue 75 (OT)
March 30, 2019 • Louisville, Kentucky

FINALLY A FINAL FOUR!

U. Va. makes Final Four after dramatically knocking off Purdue

By Norm Wood

Within seconds of the conclusion of top-seeded Virginia's 80-75 overtime win Saturday night against No. 3 seed Purdue in the NCAA tournament's South Regional final, Cavaliers forward Mamadi Diakite stood in front of the scorer's table bellowing at the top of his lungs: "Let's goooo! Let's goooooo!"

U.Va. is indeed going — back to where it's waited 35 years to return. Back to the Final Four, and it wouldn't have happened without Diakite's heroics.

Standing just outside the lane about 12 feet from the basket, his shot off a long pass from Kihei Clark as time expired in regulation tied the score 70-70, saving U.Va. (33-3) on a night that saw Purdue's Carsen Edwards light up the Cavaliers' vaunted defense for 42 points.

"It was all cold blood," Diakite said of his mindset as he took the shot. "I just grabbed it and trusted my instincts."

Virginia, which turned the ball over just five times while extending its single-season school record for wins, will play Saturday in Minneapolis, Minn., against Auburn.

Diakite, who had 14 points, seven rebounds and four blocks, helped set up the final shot in regulation, keeping the ball alive off a missed free throw. U.Va.'s Ty Jerome made the first of two free throws with 5.9 seconds left to trim Purdue's lead to 70-68, but he missed the second one.

Extending his arms above the mass of humanity in the middle of the lane after Jerome's miss, Diakite tapped the ball back out beyond midcourt. Clark chased it down and rocketed a one-armed pass to Diakite, who gathered the ball above his head with a second left, quickly lofting a shot over the reach of 7-foot-3 center Matt Haarms.

"Ty was clapping (for the ball)," U.Va. coach Tony Bennett said of the final sequence in regulation. "I was like, 'Throw it to Ty. We'll get one up there.' Mamadi, to catch it and get it off that quick — so improbable. … I was almost in shock a little bit."

Perhaps the only element of the game more stunning than Diakite's shot was Edwards' dominance.

Powered by a 10-of-19 shooting effort from 3-point range, Edwards' game represented one of the best performances in NCAA tournament history. He finished one 3-pointer shy of tying the single-game tournament record, but he did establish a regional record and connected on more 3-pointers against U.Va. than any other player in history.

The last time a player scored 40 or more points against U.Va. was Jan. 28, 2006, when Duke's J.J. Redick had exactly 40. Edwards did it while being guarded primarily by Clark and Hunter, U.Va.'s best on-ball defender and the ACC's Defensive Player of the Year, respectively.

"That was the best performance I've ever played against," said Jerome, who had 24 points and a game-

Ty Jerome (11) celebrates with teammates Mamadi Diakite (25) and De'Andre Hunter (12) after defeating Purdue 80-75 in overtime.

high seven assists. "I don't know. Kihei and (Hunter) are both great on-ball defenders, and (Edwards) just hit everything — going to the basket, step-back 3s. Unbelievable. I told him after the game that he's a hell of a player."

Edwards, who scored 24 points in the second half, was unstoppable no matter where he shot the ball — and he made a habit of shooting from long distance.

U.Va., paced by Kyle Guy's 25 points and 10 rebounds, looked to be on the verge of pulling away in the second half, building a 45-37 lead with under 14 minutes left.

Yet, Edwards responded by making 3-pointers on three consecutive possessions.

His biggest 3-pointer came with 1:10 left in regulation and Purdue (26-10) trailing 67-66. Rising up from the right side of the arc with Clark's hand in his face, Edwards banked in a 3 for a 69-67 lead and setting up the frenetic final minute.

"He's the baddest man I've ever seen," Diakite said. "I've seen (Duke's) Zion (Williamson) and all that, but a

Opposite: U.Va. players lift the South Region championship trophy, Final Four-bound for the first time in 35 years. Above: Head coach Tony Bennett cuts down the net after his team's Elite Eight win in Louisville.

guy like (Edwards), we had to double him all the time."

Nobody else on Purdue's roster scored more than seven points. Edwards' 42 points were the most scored against U.Va. in tournament history, surpassing 39 points by North Carolina's Al Wood in 1981.

"I just felt pretty comfortable," said Edwards, a 6-foot-1 junior who also scored 42 points in a second-round win against Villanova. "Never do I feel like I need to carry the team. … Never do I feel like I'm choosing to carry the team. It's just I felt good and had rhythm on the shots I was taking."

Guy snapped out of a tournament-long 3-point shooting slump in the second half. Going 5 of 12 from long range for the game, he made his first three 3-pointers of the night in the opening five minutes of the second half, helping the Cavaliers turn a 30-29 halftime deficit into a 41-34 edge and igniting his 19-point second half.

Before his second-half binge, he was 3 of 29 from 3-point range in the tournament. He twisted his right ankle with 2:09 left in the first half and had to get treatment before returning just before halftime.

"If I had known all I had to do was sprain my ankle to hit a couple shots, I would've done that a lot sooner," Guy said. "When that happened, I was pretty scared. I heard it pop … luckily, it's just a bad sprain. When I came out of halftime, I wanted to reassert my aggressiveness and shoot with as much confidence as possible, because that's what I'm known for. That's why I love these guys so much — they kept passing to me."

Coming on the 10-year anniversary of Bennett's hiring, U.Va.'s win put a series of disappointments in recent NCAA tournaments to rest, including last year's first-round loss to No. 16 seed UMBC.

"It's a pretty good 10-year anniversary gift, for sure," Bennett said.

"I'm so thankful. I don't deserve the credit. I don't care about the critics. I don't even pay attention to that. I really don't. I just know it was really hard to lose in the first round (to UMBC). It stung. It was, as I said, a painful gift. It was so humbling, but it drew me and drew our team closer in a way we couldn't have gone." ■

ACC Defensive Player of the Year De'Andre Hunter dribbles past Purdue's Grady Eifert during the first half of the South Regional final game.

Always in the mix, Virginia's Ty Jerome shoots over Purdue's Matt Haarms en route to a thrilling overtime win. After the disappointing showing in the previous year's NCAA tournament, U.Va. showed it was firmly on the march to redemption.